Avril Lavigne

by Yvonne Ventresca

LUCENT BOOKS

An imprint of Thomson Gale, a part of The Thomson Corporation

THOMSON

™

GALE

Detroit • New York • San Francisco
New Haven, Conn. • Waterville, Maine • London

LIBRARY OF CONGRESS CATALOGING-IN-PUBLICATION DATA

Ventresca, Yvonne.
  Avril Lavigne / by Yvonne Ventresca.
    p. cm. — (People in the news)
  Includes bibliographical references and index.
  ISBN 13: 978-1-59018-932-0 (hard cover : alk. paper)
  ISBN 10: 1-59018-932-9 (hard cover : alk. paper)
    1. Lavigne, Avril--Juvenile literature. 2. Singers--Canada--Biography--Juvenile literature. I. Title. II. Series: People in the news (San Diego, Calif.).
  ML3930.L25V46 2006
  782.42166092--dc22
  [B]   2006011196

Printed in the United States of America

Contents

F ame and celebrity are alluring. People are drawn to those who walk in fame's spotlight, whether they are known for great accomplishments or for notorious deeds. The lives of the famous pique public interest and attract attention, perhaps because their experiences seem in some ways so different from, yet in other ways so similar to, our own.

Newspapers, magazines, and television regularly capitalize on this fascination with celebrity by running profiles of famous people. For example, television programs such as *Entertainment Tonight* devote all of their programming to stories about entertainment and entertainers. Magazines such as *People* fill their pages with stories of the private lives of famous people. Even newspapers, newsmagazines, and television news frequently delve into the lives of well-known personalities. Despite the number of articles and programs, few provide more than a superficial glimpse at their subjects.

Lucent's People in the News series offers young readers a deeper look into the lives of today's newsmakers, the influences that have shaped them, and the impact they have had in their fields of endeavor and on other people's lives. The subjects of the series hail from many disciplines and walks of life. They include authors, musicians, athletes, political leaders, entertainers, entrepreneurs, and others who have made a mark on modern life and who, in many cases, will continue to do so for years to come.

These biographies are more than factual chronicles. Each book emphasizes the contributions, accomplishments, or deeds that have brought fame or notoriety to the individual and shows how that person has influenced modern life. Authors portray their subjects in a realistic, unsentimental light. For example, Bill Gates—the cofounder and chief executive officer of the software giant Microsoft—has been instrumental in making personal computers the most vital tool of the modern age. Few dispute his business savvy, his perseverance, or his technical expertise, yet critics say he is ruthless in his dealings with competitors and driven more by his desire to maintain Microsoft's dominance in the computer industry than by an interest in furthering technology.

In these books, young readers will encounter inspiring stories about real people who achieved success despite enormous obstacles. Oprah Winfrey—the most powerful, most watched, and wealthiest woman on television today—spent the first six years of her life in the care of her grandparents while her unwed mother sought work and a better life elsewhere. Her adolescence was colored by promiscuity, pregnancy at age fourteen, rape, and sexual abuse.

Each author documents and supports his or her work with an array of primary and secondary source quotations taken from diaries, letters, speeches, and interviews. All quotes are footnoted to show readers exactly how and where biographers derive their information and provide guidance for further research. The quotations enliven the text by giving readers eyewitness views of the life and accomplishments of each person covered in the People in the News series.

In addition, each book in the series includes photographs, annotated bibliographies, timelines, and comprehensive indexes. For both the casual reader and the student researcher, the People in the News series offers insight into the lives of today's newsmakers—people who shape the way we live, work, and play in the modern age.

A Star with Staying Power

The life of Avril Lavigne would be a dream come true for many aspiring singers: The head of a major recording studio discovers a small-town girl. She records her first album, *Let Go*, which skyrockets up the charts. Within two months, her debut goes platinum, meaning that 1 million copies have been sold in the United States alone. Within a year, *Let Go* sells 6 million U.S. copies, giving it multiplatinum status. A second multiplatinum album, *Under My Skin*, follows, along with fashion photo spreads, movie roles, and numerous awards.

If this were a fairy tale, then Lavigne might be expected to be a princess of sorts. Throughout her remarkable rise to fame, however, the former Canadian tomboy has remained less like royalty and more like a talented singer who simply loves to perform. Her childhood experiences, such as playing hockey with the boys, singing in the church choir, and even being the victim of bullying, somehow merged to create a self-assured adult.

Some parts of fame seemed to surprise her, like the endless interviews she often grumbled through, or the suggestions that she wear clothes that were more revealing. By the time Lavigne achieved celebrity status, she was no stranger to controversy. Her songwriting ability, her image, and her authenticity as an artist all came into question.

Throughout it all, she was a girl who spoke her mind. Whether she was fighting for the title of her CD or blasting other artists for lip-synching, she seemed to possess an extraor-

Avril Lavigne performs at a concert in New York City in 2002. Her CDs have sold millions of copies.

dinary amount of self-confidence, along with an uncanny ability to make solid career choices.

Of course, not every critic loved Lavigne's music or her performances. But regardless of the critical reviews, Lavigne seems to have a plan to stick around for a while. As she matured, she was not afraid to change and try new things, as shown by her transformation from skater-girl-next-door to Gucci-wearing glamorous grown-up.

Only time will tell Lavigne's future in stardom. Larry LeBlanc, *Billboard* magazine's international bureau chief in Canada, certainly feels that she has staying power. "You'll see others fade away," LeBlanc says. "Avril Lavigne won't fade away."[1]

Chapter One

Preparing for Stardom

From the time Avril Lavigne was a young girl, she always aspired to be a singer. She spent much of her childhood pursuing that goal. At sixteen years old, Avril had the chance to turn her dreams of stardom into reality.

Her opportunity came when she was able to perform for the head of a major record company. A talent scout from Arista Records had arranged for Antonio "L.A." Reid to hear Avril sing in a Manhattan recording studio. Reid had been instrumental in giving other stars, such as Pink, their big breaks. Avril might not have known much about the business side of the music industry, but she knew Reid could give her what she wanted: the opportunity to make her own CD.

As the time for her performance neared, others in the studio grew increasingly nervous about meeting Reid. Not Avril. When he arrived, she sat cross-legged on a stool and sang with confidence. Three songs later, Reid had made his decision. He offered her a record deal worth more than a million dollars that night. Avril had been preparing for that moment for much of her life.

Childhood Dreams

Avril Lavigne was born on September 27, 1984, in Belleville, Ontario. Avril's father, John, worked for the phone company Bell Canada as a network technician. Her mother, Judy, stayed home with the children: Avril, the middle child; Matt, almost two years older; and Michelle, three years younger. Avril and her family moved to Napanee, Ontario, when she was five years old.

Napanee seems like an unlikely place for a rock-pop superstar to hail from. This little town is located in a farming county about halfway between Toronto and Montreal, and country music is popular there. With a population of only five thousand people, Napanee is smaller than some of the crowds Avril would play for when she was eighteen.

Her mother first discovered her daughter's love of singing when Avril was a young child. One memory in particular stands out for Judy. She recalls rocking Avril on her lap in the living room, singing "Jesus Loves Me," and being delighted when Avril began to sing along. Although they recognized her talent before she had even started kindergarten, John and Judy knew they would have to make their own opportunities for Avril in Napanee.

The Lavignes were a devoutly religious family, and it was through their church that Avril began to hone her vocal skills.

This farmhouse in southern Ontario, Canada, is located in the area where Avril was born in 1984.

The Lavigne family had joined Evangel Temple after moving to Napanee, and Judy helped organize a children's choir there. When Avril was seven years old, this choir provided her first chance to perform with a group in public. The choir also gave her the opportunity to sing for an audience twice a week. "Avril was always looking for attention," says her brother, "and in church, she got it."[2]

Even when she was not participating in choir activities and rehearsals, Avril loved to perform. She never took voice lessons, but she annoyed her younger sister with her constant singing, often keeping her awake at night. She practiced singing in the mirror, as many kids do. As a star in the making, however, Avril took her performances a step further: She would imagine herself surrounded by cameras, and she would pretend to interview herself as though she was already famous.

Avril asked to perform solos at church and was allowed to do so when she was ten. Dressed as an angel, complete with a gold tinsel halo, she sang "Near to the Heart of God" at the church's Christmas concert. Avril gave an impressive performance for someone her age, and the resulting praise and encouragement led her to think beyond the choir. Soon after her solo, she began singing at country fairs and competing in local talent shows.

The Tomboy Choirgirl

In the choir, Avril was a girl with a sweet-sounding voice. Outside church, she was a definite tomboy and participated in a number of sports. Avril idolized her older brother, Matt, and she enthusiastically learned the sports that he liked to compete in. "If he played hockey, I had to play hockey. He played baseball, I wanted to. . . . I'm just not a girlie girl,"[3] she said of her tomboy ways.

She also played soccer, hunted, fished, and rode dirt bikes, but hockey was her favorite sport. After learning the basics from Matt, Avril played on the boys' team in the local hockey league when she was ten and eleven. She primarily played right wing, and performed so well that she was named Most Valuable Player two years in a row.

As a child, Avril liked to participate in the same sports as her brother, including hockey.

Avril was the only girl on the team, but she refused to let that stop her from joining the fray if a scuffle broke out. Her father, John, remembers wondering which troublemaker started a fight one day as the two teams left the ice. It turned out to be his own daughter, who was defending one of her teammates from an insult. Another time, Avril punched the goalie, a boy who Matt said gave her a hard time at school. Her father recorded the fight with his video camera, complete with encouraging shouts of "Avril!" from her supporters in the background.

A Change in Schools

Although Avril was tough on the ice, she was having problems at school. She was more interested in playing sports with the boys than doing things the other girls liked to do, and her female classmates did not appreciate her tomboy ways. Elementary

The Early Life of Avril Lavigne

Canada

Ontario

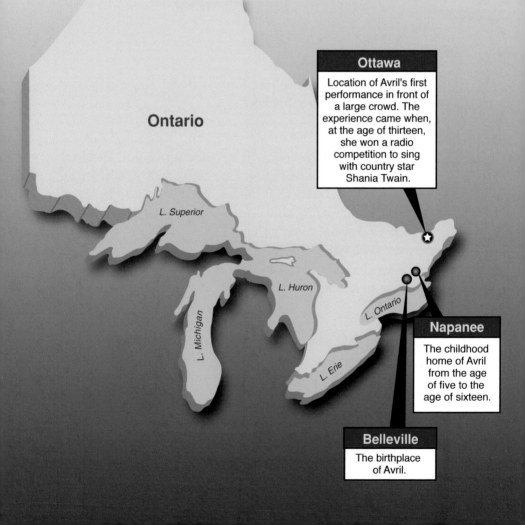

Ontario

L. Superior

L. Huron

L. Michigan

L. Ontario

L. Erie

Ottawa

Location of Avril's first performance in front of a large crowd. The experience came when, at the age of thirteen, she won a radio competition to sing with country star Shania Twain.

Napanee

The childhood home of Avril from the age of five to the age of sixteen.

Belleville

The birthplace of Avril.

school at Westdale Park Public School was rough for her, and became even more so when other girls began to harass her.

Her mother attributes the bullying to jealousy, and to avoid it, her parents switched her to a different school during the fifth grade. "She got into too many fights, so she went to a Christian school,"[4] her sister explains about Avril's transfer to Cornerstone Christian Academy, a religious private school that had recently opened nearby. Offering classes from kindergarten through eighth grade, the school had just twenty-seven students. Avril's parents hoped their daughter would thrive in this environment.

Avril flourished at Cornerstone. She made friends with another girl, Chelsea Doreen, and the two sang in school musicals together. Activities involving religion were also a big part of attending Cornerstone. School officials recall that Avril "was an enthusiastic and jovial girl, who eagerly participated in all aspects of school life. Avril was always eager to involve herself in school ministries. She read scripture to Seniors . . . and toured local churches with her classmates, singing, reciting, and testifying."[5]

Family Support

Outside of church and school, Avril soon tired of singing the religious songs that made up her repertoire. Yet even as she moved away from spiritual music, her religious parents still influenced her choice of songs. They exposed her to few musical genres besides country, and when she sang at community events and competed in talent shows, she performed only songs her parents considered acceptable. They did not allow her to sing the song "Strawberry Wine," for example, because of the reference to alcohol. The elder Lavignes were determined that their daughter not be seen as someone with loose morals. "She protected my image,"[6] Avril says about her mother's nixing that song from her performances as a young child.

Her close-knit family encouraged Avril as she indulged her love of music. Judy recalls that supporting her involved sacrifices: "We got her a sound machine with instrumental soundtracks for her to sing along with; she [practiced] continually. Then we'd get to the event and have to buy our own hamburgers."[7]

Growing Up in a Regular Home

Despite growing up with a loving family in a middle-class neighborhood, Avril had a typical childhood concern: earning some spending money. For four summers beginning at age twelve, she cut neighborhood lawns on a weekly basis for about fifteen dollars each. An occasional twenty-dollar payment seemed like a lot of money to Avril at the time. She explains: "I come from just a regular home, you know? Not really having too much money or not being able to travel or do anything. I always had hand me down clothes."

One thing her home did not include was numerous CDs, which Avril considered too expensive. She listened to some of her brother's records, such as those by the Goo Goo Dolls, but mostly listened to the contemporary female country singers her parents liked, such as Shania Twain, Faith Hill, and the Dixie Chicks.

Quoted in MuchMusic.com, "Transcript: Intimate and Interactive," May 28, 2004. www.MuchMusic.com/music/artists/transcripts.asp?artist=11&transcript=2.

Still, the practice and the exposure Avril gained at these venues was invaluable.

Other Talents

Music was also part of Avril's school experience at Cornerstone Christian Academy, as she visited other churches to sing with her classmates. In addition, Cornerstone gave her the chance to act, and she landed starring roles in three of the school's musicals.

At twelve years old, Avril decided to pursue acting away from school and she auditioned at a nearby community theater. Local theater director Tim Picotte was managing a production of the musical *You're a Good Man, Charlie Brown*. Avril impressed Picotte so much that he created a part for her as Charlie Brown's younger sister, Sally. She worked with him again two years later in *Godspell*, in which she played a rebellious teenager. Picotte recalls that even back then Avril was confident about meeting her goals. "I think she probably told us the first week," he says. "She was going to be a star."[8]

Besides acting, Avril also prepared for stardom by teaching herself to play the guitar. Although piano lessons had failed to excite her as a child, learning the guitar was another matter. Between the ages of about twelve and fourteen, she gradually taught herself by playing the same songs repeatedly on her father's guitar. For example, she played rocker Lenny Kravitz's hit "Fly Away" until she had it down pat. Over time, she became more proficient and experimented with writing her own music, such as a song called "Can't Stop Thinking about You," about a teenage crush.

First Recording

Avril's focus on music and singing continued, and in 1999 she sang on her first CD. The break came from Stephen Medd, a family friend and a local folk musician. Medd had heard Avril in a community performance, and the two had sung together at a local event, the Quinte Spirit Festival. Impressed with her talent, he asked her to sing on the CD he was producing. She sang backup vocals on two songs: "World to Me," and the title track, "The Quinte Spirit." Her main contribution, however, was the lead vocal on a country-gospel song called "Touch the Sky," which Medd had written especially to showcase her abilities.

Before the recording session, Avril had just a week to practice. Medd recalls being amazed that the song was recorded in a single take. "This is a 14-year-old girl, never been in a studio, walks in like a pro and nailed it," he says. "It completely stunned me."[9]

Despite her talent, Avril went through a period of not wanting to perform. Opportunities for singing publicly were limited in Napanee. The crowds at country fairs were frequently small and the mixed-age groups did not always appreciate Avril's talents. Tired of playing for unenthusiastic audiences, Avril started to limit her appearances. Her mother often had to make up excuses to get her out of attending events. At fourteen, however, Avril had the chance to sing in front of an enormous crowd, and that performance changed the momentum of her career.

Sharing the Spotlight with Shania

In 1999 during country-pop superstar Shania Twain's "Come On Over" tour, an Ottawa radio station invited listeners to send in recordings of themselves singing "What Made You Say That," one of Twain's hit songs. The winner would go onstage and sing a duet with Twain during her concert at the Corel Centre in Kanata, Ontario, a suburb of Ottawa.

Because of a mix-up with the dates, Avril almost missed the contest deadline. The night before it was due to be submitted, she completed her recording of the song. The Lavignes rushed the tape to the radio station in a paper bag.

The radio station chose Avril's recording as the contest winner out of hundreds of entries. A few days later, she joined Twain onstage during the concert. She told Twain and about twenty thousand of Twain's fans that she wanted to be a famous singer. Then, with incredible confidence, Avril sang "What Made You Say That" with Twain. She received a standing ovation.

Performing in the spotlight before such a large, enthusiastic audience revived Avril's commitment to music. "She really took off after that,"[10] observes her mother. Avril knew, more than ever, that singing was what she wanted to do.

More School Blues

While her music was progressing, Avril's high school life was not going as smoothly. She graduated from the Cornerstone Christian Academy, which offered classes only through the eighth grade. She ended on a positive note, receiving two awards. One was for the most improved graduate, the other for her musical abilities.

Then Avril started ninth grade at Napanee District Secondary School, transferring from a school with well under a hundred

Shania Twain

Like Avril Lavigne, Shania Twain was raised in a small Canadian town. Twain was named Eilleen Regina Edwards at birth, but used the name Eilleen Twain when her mother remarried an Ojibwa man, Jerry Twain.

When Twain was in her early twenties, her mother and stepfather died in a car accident. Shania performed at a local resort to support her sister and two brothers. An entertainment lawyer from Nashville discovered her a few years later, which led to a country record deal with Mercury Nashville Records. When the record label asked her to change her last name, she decided to change her first name instead. Shania means "I'm on my way" in Ojibwa.

Twain's CD *Come On Over* has sold over 34 million copies worldwide, making it the best-selling album by a female solo artist. She also released *Up!* in 2002 and her *Greatest Hits* in 2004.

Popular country singer Shania Twain was born and raised in Canada.

students to one with over a thousand. Her new school featured many cliques—small groups of students who dressed and talked alike and who tended to exclude anyone who dared to be different. Avril quickly found that she did not fit in with any of her high school's defined social groups. Although she wanted to be friends with the "preps," more well-off teens who hoped to go to exclusive private colleges, they rejected her attempts at friendship. After dealing with these popularity issues over time, she began to worry less about other people's opinions. "I just started being myself and dressing the way I wanted to,"[11] she says.

About the same time she quit worrying about befriending the preppy kids, Avril finally found where she fit in. She learned how to skateboard, and during tenth grade began associating with other skateboarders. With her new group of friends supporting her, she was able to stand up for herself in a convincing way, and she could be intimidating despite her small size. Although she stood barely over five feet tall (1.5m), Avril projected an air of confidence after finding her niche.

Getting Discovered

Avril's confidence served her well, and her self-esteem helped impress professional music manager Cliff Fabri. He first met Avril when he heard her singing country songs in November 1999. His company, RomanLine Entertainment, was based in Kingston, Ontario, not far from Napanee, and she was performing at the Chapters bookstore there to promote Medd's CD.

Avril accepted Fabri's offer to manage her; he would advise her on creative and business decisions relating to her music career. At that time, Avril was still evolving as a musician and deciding what genres of music appealed to her. Fabri felt her strict upbringing had sheltered her from many types of music. As her first manager, Fabri exposed her to various musical artists and styles and explained the music business. "We worked on everything,"[12] he says.

Fabri also encouraged Avril to continue writing her own songs. Fabri felt that the ability to write was a key skill for musical artists. Songwriting not only made their music unique, it

Avril mugs for the camera with her brother Matt (left) and first manager Cliff Fabri (right). Fabri met Avril in 1999.

also made money. It was more profitable for musicians to have songwriting credits, instead of merely performing someone else's songs.

Under Fabri's guidance, Avril found more opportunities to perform. He arranged shows and appearances in Napanee and the surrounding area. She still primarily sang country songs, but also added to her repertoire a noncountry song, "Kiss Me," by the band Sixpence None the Richer.

After mentioning her to people in the music industry, Fabri was ready to launch Avril in 2000. He created a video of her performing and sent it to talent scouts at various record labels. Part of his efforts included attending the annual North By Northeast music conference in Toronto with her that June. Fabri

Pink

Before L.A. Reid discovered Avril, he signed another young up-and-coming female singer known as Pink. Born Alecia Moore, Pink had a short stint with an R&B group, then sang in another band called Choice. Choice got a record deal from LaFace Records, which was cofounded by L.A. Reid and Kenneth "Babyface" Edmonds.

The group Choice did not last, but Reid offered Pink the opportunity to make a solo album. LaFace Records released her debut CD, *Can't Take Me Home,* in 2000 and it has sold 6 million copies worldwide. Her second CD, *M!ssundaztood,* was even more commercially successful and sold 11 million copies.

In 2002 Avril was one of the presenters when Pink won MTV's Best Female Video Award for "Get the Party Started," a song from her second CD. Avril and Pink together have estimated combined CD sales worth over $250 million.

Pink is a successful singer and has sold millions of CDs.

arranged for Avril to meet with, rather than perform for, a few record company representatives, and she made some key industry contacts.

One of those contacts was Ken Krongard, a talent scout for Arista Records. Without even hearing her perform, Krongard felt that Avril had the right look to be a successful teen singer. Another key contact came through the videotapes Fabri had sent out. Mark Jowett of Nettwerk Records was impressed with Avril's talent.

Nettwerk Records decided to take a chance on the teenager and offered her a development deal. A typical development deal helps an artist pursue a career by providing things like recording studio access and funding. In exchange, if a record deal comes through, the company usually receives a percentage of the profits. The first step in Avril's development deal involved going to New York City in the fall of 2000.

Bright Lights, Big City

As part of the development deal, Nettwerk introduced her to producer-songwriter Peter Zizzo, and she traveled back and forth from Napanee to New York several times for musical sessions with him. Avril learned some of Zizzo's songs, and collaborated with him to write "Why," a melodic song with an acoustic guitar that showcased Avril's vocal talent. Fabri considered "Why" a turning point in his young client's development because it helped prove Avril's songwriting skills. In addition, it gave her more confidence in her ability to write. At this point, Avril's musical style seemed to be heading toward country.

During one of Avril and Zizzo's sessions in October, Krongard came by the recording studio. Awed by Avril's performance, he arranged for her to return to New York the following week and sing for L.A. Reid, who had recently taken over as the head of Arista Records.

Zizzo admits to being nervous that night, but Avril, never one to have stage fright, seemed unfazed by Reid's presence. She fearlessly sang two songs Zizzo had written for country-crossover singer Faith Hill, then she ended with "Why." After

In 2000 Avril celebrated her new contract with Arista Records at the Windows on the World restaurant in New York City.

a difficult workday in his new role at Arista, Reid had walked into the recording studio feeling irritated. But Avril's performance transformed his mood, and he decided on the spot to sign her.

Although the actual contract would take time to finalize, Avril had gotten her big break. That evening, Reid sent a limousine to take the group out to dinner. They celebrated at Windows on the World, the famous restaurant that overlooked Manhattan from the top of the World Trade Center. Avril received a $1.25 million, two-album contract based on the vocals for three songs she sang that night.

"It was her voice and her songwriting," says Reid, explaining what sold him on Avril. "And she's a dynamite-looking girl with an amazing attitude."[13] Avril Lavigne, just sixteen years old, was about to fulfill her childhood dream of becoming a musical star.

Chapter Two

A Complicated CD

If getting a record deal had seemed easy for Avril, actually making a debut album was a complex undertaking. She was still defining her sound, and her initial tracks were not in the musical style Arista executives expected. Avril persuaded the people at her record label to accept her switch to the pop-rock genre. She soon developed a pattern of controversial outspokenness both at the record company and, after the CD's release, with the press.

Away from Home

Before Avril could deal with the people at Arista, she first had to resolve a controversy at home. It began after L.A. Reid arranged for her to begin working on her album in Manhattan. Creating her debut CD in New York, however, would make it impossible for the sixteen-year-old to continue attending her local high school. "We encouraged her to take correspondence [for high school credit] and she was totally against it,"[14] Judy Lavigne says.

Much to her parents' disappointment, Avril decided to drop out of school altogether, with no immediate plan to work toward her diploma. Her contract with Arista was a "once in a life-time opportunity,"[15] Avril says. If her musical career did not take off, she felt she could always return to school and complete her education.

With her decision about school behind her, Avril was eager to begin work on the CD. But the Lavignes were reluctant to let

Avril (second from right) and her family proudly pose with her new record contract in 2001.

her move to New York alone. Her brother, Matt, decided to temporarily relocate with her, to serve as an informal chaperone. The two left Napanee for an apartment in New York's Greenwich Village in January 2001. Avril's record deal with Arista took care of the pricey rent. Without school and money to worry about, there would be nothing to distract her from her music.

Finding the Right Sound

After Avril set out to begin her debut CD, one complication arose immediately: She wanted to write her own songs. Even though Avril's recording contract was for singing, not songwriting, she asked the record company to let her write as well. "There's nothing wrong with [other people's ballads], but it wasn't me,"[16] she says.

The record company agreed to let her write, but Arista executives wanted to give her assistance. They introduced her to some established Manhattan-based songwriters and asked her to collaborate with them. Such an arrangement is not unusual in the music industry. Still, after several months, Avril was unhappy with the type of songs being created.

In some ways, Avril's successful audition began to work against her. Reid had signed Avril for her singing talent, but he also expected the new country or country-crossover sound he had heard initially. Avril's musical interests had clearly evolved. In an article for *Entertainment Weekly*, Chris Willman described Avril at this point as someone "who'd just discovered guitar-based rock."[17]

Although she had listened to country artists like Faith Hill and the Dixie Chicks when she was younger, her explorations into other types of music now led her to pursue more of a pop-rock direction. She later explained to *Girls' Life* magazine that country music "does not suit my personality."[18]

Leaving New York

After unsuccessfully attempting to work with other producers and writers in New York City, Avril was about five months into her contract without having written even one song. "I think the record company was getting worried or [angry]," Fabri, her manager recalls because Avril was rejecting the songs presented to her. Although he and Avril "accepted that we needed help [songwriting], the material just wasn't what we had decided she was going to put out."[19]

The pressure was starting to mount. Avril and Fabri realized that if she had no songs to record, the label could drop her, and her dreams of stardom could come to an abrupt end. They decided the best approach would be to leave New York and get a fresh start with some songwriters in California. Arista set up their first meeting, which resulted in another disappointing experience. Once again, there was a failure to connect with her developing musical style. Avril's frustration increased, and Fabri knew they had to try something different. Through an industry contact, he arranged to meet with Clif Magness, another songwriter and producer in California.

Magness did not have any information about Avril from Arista, and that turned out to be an asset. Without any preconceived ideas about Avril from the record company, Magness became the partner she needed. After their first working session together, Magness and Avril had created "Unwanted," a rock-style song about parents rejecting their son's girlfriend.

Something between Avril and Magness had clicked, but Fabri predicted that the record company would not like the results. He was right. A label executive listened to "Unwanted," but initially did not think a rock song belonged on Avril's album.

Connecting with the Matrix

After criticizing the musical style of "Unwanted," Arista executives suggested in May 2001 that Avril meet with the Matrix, a trio of songwriters/producers. The record label had contacted them ahead of time, and they had already written a song for Avril at Arista's request. Once again, though, Avril refused to record something that she had no part in creating.

But this time, Avril could provide a concrete example of what she wanted to do musically. Fabri brought along a recording of "Unwanted" to their meeting with the Matrix and used it to demonstrate her musical style. Avril and the Matrix began working on a new song together, and in an afternoon, the song titled "Complicated" was born. This pop song had potential to become a huge hit, which pleased the record company, and it was closer to the style of music Avril wanted to make. For the first time since she signed her contract, Avril and the record company were both happy with the results.

Confidence and Control

Despite his help in getting her CD started, within weeks of creating "Complicated," Avril replaced Fabri as her manager. The missteps in creating her debut album were a likely cause for ending their relationship. She hired Nettwerk, the company that had arranged her first trip to New York City in the fall, to take over the management of her career. With new management and a new song, Avril was prepared to complete her first album. "Complicated" served as the spark that she needed, and the rest of the songs came together soon after.

By the time her efforts with the CD were finished, Avril had convinced Arista to let her move away from the music they had expected based on her audition and into the world of pop-rock. While "Complicated" could be categorized as pop, other songs from her CD, such as "Losing Grip" and "Unwanted," fell more into the rock spectrum.

After changing genres, Avril still had other battles to fight. One was over the CD's title. Reid wanted to name it after a track she created with the Matrix, "Anything but Ordinary." Avril had her own ideas, however, which resulted in many phone calls back and forth with Arista. Avril finally called Reid directly and convinced him to call it *Let Go*. It was a bold move for a debut artist, but speaking out cemented her right to influence the resulting CD.

Lauren Christy (right) was part of the songwriting team for Avril's first CD.

Avril asserted control again when the engineers made the finishing changes to the CD during the production process. She felt they had added too many computerized drum noises and that the album sounded too pop and less rock-oriented as a result. She flew to Los Angeles to speak with the producers in person, and talked to them about changing the production. After meeting with her, they agreed to make the sound edgier, as she requested.

The Original Touring Band

Let Go took more than eighteen months to complete, but the work was not yet over. Avril still needed a band to perform on the road with her. As her touring band, these were not the same musicians that recorded the actual CD, but they would be included on the CD's credits and they would play her songs in concert.

It was important to Avril that her future bandmates be young, and she got her wish. The musicians heard about her through

Clif Magness (left) worked with Avril to create the song "Unwanted" for her debut CD.

word of mouth, particularly through the Canadian band Sum 41, which Nettwerk also managed. Mark Spicoluk had played briefly with Sum 41 before starting his own band, Closet Monster. He was building up his own punk record label, Underground Operations, before joining Avril as her bassist. Spicoluk later recruited Jesse Colburn, another member of Closet Monster, to play rhythm guitar.

Drummer Matthew Brann also heard about the opportunity through friends in Sum 41. At first he was not sure about joining a band with a female lead singer. He decided to sign up, however, after hearing "Complicated," meeting Avril, and rehearsing with her a few times. Brann says, "I realized . . . that she had that real star quality about her."[20]

Evan Taubenfeld had graduated from high school and had been accepted at the Berklee College of Music in Boston before joining Avril's group. After hearing about the opportunity from a friend at Arista, Taubenfeld learned her songs in three days and landed the job as her lead guitarist.

Avril was pleased with the resulting band. "They're not just like hired musicians standing there behind me just playing. . . . We have something really special and we connect really well,"[21] she said.

Let Go Comes Out

With the band in place, marketing efforts for the CD gained momentum. In the spring of 2002, Avril went on a six-week tour with Taubenfeld before *Let Go* was released in stores. Their live shows, in which they performed songs from the upcoming CD, helped build excitement among fans.

Avril's management also arranged online opportunities to help create demand for her music. AOL Music's Artist Discovery Network debuted "Complicated" in March. Before the single was even released to radio stations, the song was requested 350,000 times online within a month.

Another piece of marketing involved the music video for "Complicated," which came out about two months before the CD. The video visually introduced Avril, showing her riding

Avril and her bandmates take time to clown around during a promotional tour in 2002.

a skateboard and playfully hanging around a mall with her band. Her baggy pants, sneakers, and tough-girl expression combined with her skateboarding helped define her image as a skater punk. Her unique identity and fun video further promoted her debut CD.

Arista released *Let Go* in stores on June 4, 2002. The CD hit *Billboard*'s Top 10 within weeks after its release, as teens connected with Avril's songs and style. "Complicated" received a lot of radio play. Race Taylor, a DJ for the prominent New York radio station WPLJ, explains Avril's appeal:

> The thing with Avril is that she burst onto the scene very much at a time where she was unlike anything else that was out there. Everyone was completely saturated with Britney and Christina. . . . Avril Lavigne stood on her own. She probably had a persona and an attitude that was more identifiable to the American public than these other artists were, and it would be very easy to see why young teenage girls in particular would gravitate towards her. There was a

rock edge that was maybe nonexistent for people her age at that point in time.[22]

A Sense of Style

As "Complicated" climbed the charts, Avril did magazine photo shoots to further promote her album. She learned quickly that she would need to resist stylists' efforts to transform her into a typical pop princess. Just as she expressed her individuality through her music, she also wanted to express her true self

Avril's trademark style included baggy pants, white tank tops, and mens' ties.

through her clothes. When she went to photo shoots, she says, "they kind of [wanted] to make me more girlie and they [had] racks of clothing. . . . I'm like, 'Let me see. Nope, nope, nope, not into heels, not into pearls. I think I'll just wear what I've got on now'."[23] Cargo pants, white tank tops, and men's ties became her trademark look.

Avril's tomboyish style was decidedly low maintenance, but despite being almost antifashion, she soon became a trendsetter. As her fame grew, teenage fans began copying her low-key look. "She took that trend and brought it to the masses," says Sharon Haver, founder of FocusOnStyle.com, an online reality-based fashion magazine.

> Teenagers have a tendency to find somebody to use as their style icon, typically when they're younger. . . . What she wore was also very affordable. It wasn't like she came out wearing a Chanel studded motorcycle jacket that cost [thousands of dollars]. She was wearing a tank top that's [inexpensive], and she was wearing a tie you can take from Dad's closet. So what she had was very easy for someone to go home, not even buy anything else, and wear and look cute in.[24]

Because of Avril's influence and the affordability of the look, wearing a tie soon became a popular fashion statement among teenage girls.

The Anti-Britney Authentic Girl

In contrast with the images of pop princesses Britney Spears and Christina Aguilera, Avril's look was refreshing. There was no cleavage, no pierced belly button in sight. The press quickly dubbed her the "Anti-Britney" because both her look and her music were so different from that of Spears and other female pop stars.

Avril used the Anti-Britney label to underscore the point that she did not need revealing clothes or a sexy image to sell her records. While performing live, she wore the same type of clothes she would wear any other day, because she wanted her

Vanessa Carlton

In 2002 the press often linked Avril with Vanessa Carlton as another "authentic girl." Raised in a small Pennsylvania town, Carlton began playing piano at an early age. She studied ballet at the School of American Ballet in New York, but decided not to pursue a career in dance. While attending Columbia University, she performed her music in various Manhattan bars. After meeting Peter Zizzo, she worked with him to record a demo tape. A few months after its completion, she secured a record deal. Her debut CD, *Be Not Nobody*, was released in 2002, about a month before Avril's *Let Go*. Carlton's first hit song, "A Thousand Miles," competed against "Complicated" for the 2003 Song of the Year. Both lost the Grammy to Norah Jones's "Don't Know Why."

Vanessa Carlton's first CD was released at about the same time as Avril's.

fans to focus on her music, not the way she looked. Even in her videos, she wanted viewers, as she said in *Rolling Stone*, to "not be staring at my girl parts but to be listening to my lyrics."[25]

Some observers compared her image to that of singers Michelle Branch and Vanessa Carlton. An article linked Avril to Branch and Carlton soon after *Let Go* hit the charts, calling them "the authentic girls" because all three young women were involved in the songwriting process and created introspective lyrics. The authentic girls also downplayed glamour and highlighted their musical and songwriting abilities instead.

Image Controversy

Despite all the favorable press about Avril's genuineness, some observers disagreed. One article implied that the authentic girls' realness was as planned as the sexiness of other pop singers, with the only difference being that they were better at concealing the fact. There was suspicion that the record company had actually created Avril's seemingly down-to-earth image.

A *Rolling Stone* article in August 2002 created more speculation. In that interview, Avril spoke about getting into fights, carrying a knife after moving to New York City, and being thrown out of a hotel. A subsequent feature in the *Toronto Star* referred to her image as "skateboarding tough-talking pop-punk princess."[26]

Fabri, her former manager, fed the suspicion that Avril was not the streetwise girl she pretended to be. He denied that she had a skater punk persona when they had worked together, and said that she was "probably more contrived than Britney ever was."[27] However, others who knew her well saw Avril as a teenager who had moved from a small town to New York City, and as a result had grown and changed musically and stylistically over time. Zizzo said she had dressed in the fatigues and tank tops when he first met her, and that her confident image certainly was real.

Avril denied the accusations that the record label had anything to do with her personality or appearance. If that were true, she claimed, her look would have been far less wholesome. "I'd have bleached-blond hair and I'd probably be wearing a bra for a shirt,"[28] she said.

After Avril gained fame, some critics speculated that her tough-girl image was false.

The Semantics of Punk

The controversy did not end with the fake versus real debate. Criticism increased when it became apparent that despite the skater punk image portrayed in the media, Avril was not knowledgeable about punk music. While her hit "Complicated" reflected her dislike of people that pretend to be someone they are not, this is exactly what people in chat rooms and message boards were saying Avril herself was doing. She never listened to influential punk musicians, such as the Sex Pistols, and yet she seemed to be associating herself with the punk genre.

Avril did not think her musical background should matter. "Punk doesn't have anything to do with your music," she says.

The punk band Sex Pistols performs in 1978. Avril was criticized for projecting a punk image while not having knowledge about that style of music.

"I could be punk and have pop music."[29] She seemed to use the word "punk" more to mean a young person with an attitude than a style of music.

Still, the criticism continued. Taubenfeld says the experience was a tough one for the singer. "What hurt her the most was people calling her a fake, calling her a phony,"[30] he says. In response to the disapproval, Avril distanced herself from the term and denied being punk when interviewers used it to describe her style.

Songwriter or Not?

Although Avril dismissed the controversy over whether she was punk as a difference in semantics, she had to confront another criticism that cut close to her heart: Some said that she was not a real songwriter. One person who scoffed at her songwriting skills was the Matrix's Scott Spock. According to Spock, "Complicated" was written by Lauren Christy, Graham Edwards, and him, with little help from Avril. "Her and Lauren changed some lyrics,"[31] Spock says. Christy agreed with Spock, saying that the Matrix used guitar and piano to create the basis for the songs, and that Avril did bits of melody and some wording changes.

Avril disputes that view, saying, "Me and Lauren sat down and did all the lyrics together for every single song."[32] Edwards, she explains, worked out the guitar parts with her approval. There are no songwriting credits on *Let Go* to clarify who wrote what. Nevertheless, the Matrix had planted a seed of doubt about her songwriting ability.

Fame and Celebrations

Despite the image and songwriting controversies, and because of the publicity they generated, Avril's fame continued to grow

Members of Avril's songwriting team (pictured) claimed that she contributed little to the melodies and lyrics of her first CD.

over the summer of 2002. "Complicated" became the number-one music video on *Total Request Live (TRL)*, a popular music television show in the United States. She was also nominated for MTV Video Music Awards' Best New Artist in a Video for that song. Upon winning the award, she said, "This is amazing. My dreams are coming true."[33]

Autumn brought more celebrations when Avril turned eighteen in September. Her record label surprised her with an ice hockey birthday party at Chelsea Piers, a sports complex in Manhattan that features an indoor ice-skating rink. She showed

Avril poses for cameras at the 2002 MTV Video Music Awards, where she won Best New Artist in a Video.

off her hockey talents and knocked an Arista executive down on the ice. Avril was famous enough for *Rolling Stone* magazine to include a brief article about her party. One of her presents, the magazine noted, was a much-desired iPod.

Changes in the Band

Avril seemed to accept her new fame. "I think I have been preparing for this [fame and success] all my life. This is what I wanted. This is my dream, my goal in life, and this is what I've been working for, so I am ready!"[34] she said.

Not everyone was as happy as Avril, however. In October, Mark Spicoluk left the group. He was dissatisfied with the large amount of marketing required for Avril's music, and he returned to to his original band and the independent label he had founded. Charles Moniz, who had been part of a Toronto band called Grade, replaced Spicoluk as bassist.

Continued Success

Avril's popularity continued as two other songs from her debut CD, "Sk8er Boi" and "I'm With You," became top ten hits. By the year's end, *Let Go* had become one of the top three best-selling albums of the year and was certified as multiplatinum. Avril had successfully skyrocketed to fame during 2002. The next year would bring its own challenges as she struggled to balance her newfound celebrity with some sense of normalcy.

Chapter Three

Balancing Fame and Normalcy

A vril Lavigne's stardom gave her both advantages and aggravation. Winning awards, helping charities, and beginning a major tour came along with the fame. But the media often intruded into her personal life, through both the interviews she was required to do for public relations, and through the surprise photos that appeared in the tabloids. Lavigne tried to maintain a sense of normalcy despite her celebrity status.

Grammy Nominations

For Lavigne the year 2003 started with the announcement of the nominees for the Grammy Awards, which recognize musical excellence. Lavigne received five nominations in January, for Pop Vocal Album, Song of the Year (for "Complicated"), Best New Artist, Female Pop Vocal Performance (for "Complicated"), and Female Rock Vocal Performance (for "Sk8er Boi"). She was thrilled as she had heard the first three nominations being announced, then she learned about the additional two. Amazed and excited, Lavigne called her mother to share the news of her good fortune.

The T-Shirt Craze

Lavigne's good luck, it turned out, soon benefited others. When she was invited to appear as a musical guest on *Saturday Night*

Live in January, she chose to wear a childhood soccer T-shirt in keeping with the fashion of wearing old, or "vintage," tops. A local Home Hardware outlet had sponsored her Napanee soccer team, and the store's name appeared on the front of the shirt. After she wore the shirt on SNL, the Home Hardware chain received many requests from fans wanting to buy identical T-shirts.

The Home Hardware store in Napanee made plans to sell several hundred shirts. Within a month, fans had ordered several thousand. Over the next three years, the Home Hardware chain sold well over twenty thousand of them. The owner of Napanee's Home Hardware franchise, in turn, contributed some of

After Lavigne wore this T-shirt on television, thousands of duplicate shirts were ordered from the Home Hardware chain.

the profits to charities that Lavigne selected, including the Greater Napanee Soccer Association and the Hospital for Sick Children Foundation.

Napanee's Girl

Besides the demand for Home Hardware T-shirts, Lavigne's fame brought other recognition to her hometown of Napanee. The local pizza restaurant, La Pizzeria, named Lavigne's favorite pizza after her. (Originally made with green olives, mushrooms, and pepperoni, eventually the pizza was made without meat when Lavigne began eating more of a vegetarian diet.) Her high school became inundated with phone calls. Cornerstone Christian Academy received so many inquiries that it developed a standard press release to deal with reporters' questions. Some people traveled to visit the place where Lavigne grew up.

In general, the people of Napanee were extremely proud of their association with Lavigne. "It's the typical small-town [in] Ontario, where neighbors know neighbors and help neighbors," says former Napanee mayor David Remington. "I think it made it extra special that people knew Avril. They knew her from church, they knew her from other associations, and so it had a different feel than if maybe you were from . . . a larger community." Remington notes that the singer's fame had a positive impact on the town. "I think she inspired a lot of young kids in the community. . . . It's the cliché of dreams are possible and you can accomplish things if you really work hard."[35]

After her Grammy nominations became public, Lavigne was the first item on the agenda at the next town council meeting. The town's leaders decided to hold a party in her honor at Napanee's high school on the night of the Grammy Awards.

Worldwide Recognition

Lavigne's fame, however, was not limited to her hometown, or even to North America. She began receiving worldwide recognition as well. That January, she attended MTV's Asia Awards. She won three, including Favorite Female Artist.

Avril and Alanis

Avril Lavigne's musical style has often been compared to that of Alanis Morissette, another young Canadian singer. Before Morissette worked with producer Glen Ballard in the United States in 1994, she had released two albums in Canada. *Jagged Little Pill*, her resulting CD with Ballard, was filled with more honest, angry, and angst-ridden songs than her earlier work. She released *Jagged Little Pill* when she was just twenty-one. It went on to sell more than 30 million copies worldwide. Morissette says,

> I have always felt while writing a song . . . there is a green light for me to express the most reactive, the most embarrassing, devastated, wounded and vulnerable parts of me in a very safe and non-destructive way. This wasn't the first time I'd done it, but [the song "You Oughta Know"] connected with people to say the least, and it also offered a green light to other people.

Morissette may have turned on the green light for Lavigne, whose lyrics would become even more personal with *Under My Skin*. Lavigne has said that she found Morissette inspiring.

Quoted in Alanis Morissette Web site, "Bio," 2006. www.maverick.com/alanis.

Canadian singer Alanis Morissette (pictured) has been a big inspiration for Lavigne.

In the United States, the Grammy ceremonies were approaching, but not everyone thought she would actually receive an award. For example, Chris Willman of *Entertainment Weekly* expressed doubts about the chances of her and another nominee, Vanessa Carlton, winning. Willman felt it was too early for Lavigne to receive the honor. "[Grammy] voters [from the National Academy of Recording Arts & Sciences] will wait [until] at least Lavigne's second album before deciding whether she's Grammy material,"[36] he said.

The big night arrived in February 2003. In keeping with her character, Lavigne avoided wearing a designer gown. Instead, she and members of her band dressed in "the ugliest tuxedos they could find. On purpose,"[37] according to an MTV reporter. Lavigne completed the look with a light blue shirt and sneakers.

Back in Napanee, hundreds watched the awards show on a big-screen television at the local high school. "People just felt so good to cheer Avril on and to be a part of her experience,"[38] Remington says. When Lavigne walked the red carpet before

Lavigne and her bandmates pose for the cameras during the 2003 Grammy Awards.

the ceremony, the high school principal phoned her so she could hear the sounds of her hometown rooting for her. But Willman was right about Lavigne and Carlton. Both walked away from the ceremonies empty-handed.

"Sk8er Boi" and eBay

Despite her being shut out at the Grammys, there was no denying Lavigne's popularity. That mass appeal was something that continued to help others as well. When by chance Lavigne wore a green and gold T-shirt bearing the name of an elementary school in Wilkesboro, North Carolina, for her "Sk8er Boi" video, the school was flooded with requests from fans who wanted to buy those T-shirts. The school sold many of the shirts on the online auction site eBay and used the money to pay for new computers.

Others sought personal gain from their association with the now-famous singer. An old boyfriend from Napanee tried to sell on eBay what he claimed were love letters she had written in high school. The site removed the listing to protect Lavigne's possible copyrights after receiving a complaint from an unmentioned source. But eBay items did not necessarily need a personal connection to Lavigne for people to try auctioning them. Even rocks people had picked up in Napanee were offered for sale.

Maintaining Normalcy

The media attention, combined with her first worldwide tour, meant that Lavigne's time was rarely her own. She started her tour with a handful of North American cities, then played shows in Europe in March 2003. Although she still technically lived with her parents, most of her days were spent on the road. When *Let Go* first came out, her mother mentioned to reporters that Avril's busy schedule made it hard to reach her, and that situation continued as her fame increased. Judy Lavigne admitted to using the Internet to find news about her daughter and her new life.

When Lavigne did see her family, she was determined not to let riches and fame go to her head. For example, when her

Johnny Rzeznik

Johnny Rzeznik, guitarist and lead vocalist for the Goo Goo Dolls, is one singer Avril admires. The Goo Goo Dolls started playing in 1986, but did not achieve commercial success until 1995 with their hit single "Name." In 1998 the band was asked to write a song for the *City of Angels* movie soundtrack. The resulting song, "Iris," was a number-one hit on the *Billboard* airplay charts for several months that year.

The song was also included on the Goo Goo Dolls' 1998 CD, *Dizzy Up the Girl*. "Iris" is one of Avril's favorite songs, and in 2004 she and Rzeznik performed a surprise duet of the song at a Fashion Rocks concert.

Rzeznik has expressed admiration for the young singer and indicated he would like to work with her again in the future. "I would love to do a song for Avril Lavigne," he said.

Quoted in Brandee J. Tecson, "Goo Goo Dolls' Katrina-Relief Song Inspired by 'Unfairness in This Country,'" VH1.com, November 21, 2005. www.VH1.com/artists/news/15127 08/11012005/goo_goo_dolls.jhtml.

Goo Goo Dolls front man Johnny Rzeznik (left) has expressed a desire to write a song for Lavigne.

father teasingly suggested she buy herself a BMW convertible, she became annoyed and said she was more interested in a used Jeep. Still the frugal girl her parents had always known, she made it clear that she had not changed much since the release of her best-selling CD.

Judy Lavigne made a few trips to meet up with Avril as she toured. Her friends from Napanee also traveled to see her perform occasionally, but she did not keep in touch with many people from high school. Lavigne's new friends were primarily the members of her band and touring crew. She was particularly close to her guitarist, Evan Taubenfeld. He told reporters that when people from the media caused her trouble, "I try to just be there to support her."[39]

Lavigne and her guitarist Evan Taubenfeld (right) became close during her tour in 2003.

The Junos

Taubenfeld was there for the good times with Lavigne as well. In 2003 she was nominated for six Juno Awards, which are Canada's equivalent of the Grammys. She won four of them, for Best New Artist, Best Pop Album, Album of the Year (beating out Shania Twain's album *Up!*), and Single of the Year. Lavigne expressed joy at the positive recognition of her first album. "This is just so incredible . . . having this dream of mine come true,"[40] Lavigne told the audience.

Some noted that off-camera, however, her attitude at the Junos was less enthusiastic. One reporter commented that she was "rather endearingly, every inch the bored teenager backstage."[41] That same reporter also observed that during his interview, Lavigne chose to ignore some of his questions altogether.

Losing Interest in Interviews

Ignoring questions put to her by reporters eventually became a way for Lavigne to deal with interviews, which she came to think of as drudgery. At first, Lavigne gave interviews her best effort. Ann Marie McQueen interviewed her for the *Ottawa Sun* newspaper in the summer of 2002. She recalls that during her interview, "Avril was tired, having got in late the night before. And she seemed so unlike the bad skater girl image we'd been seeing. She seemed small, worn out. Her nails had chipped black polish; her hair was flat-ironed, and a bit greasy. She seemed very much like a kid. Shy too, she looked down a lot when she talked, at her fingers, or the floor."[42]

Lavigne still showed spunk during the interview, though. She had postponed a photo during McQueen's questions because the flash annoyed her. When her public relations representative tried to end the session before the picture was taken, she overruled him, saying that she had promised the photo. Lavigne then insisted that it be taken. McQueen says, "She's one of the better [celebrities] I've talked to over the last four years."[43]

Another interviewer noted that Lavigne was comfortable discussing men, and that she had even addressed rumors about a relationship between her and Deryck Whibley, lead singer for

Deryck Whibley of Sum 41 rehearses for a concert in 2003. During interviews, Lavigne refused to discuss her relationship with Whibley.

the band Sum 41. She admitted that they were "sort of friends,"[44] but not long afterward she adopted a strict policy of refusing to answer any questions about her personal life.

As time went on, reporters frequently commented about her moodiness and bored demeanor during interviews. Her attitude during meetings with reporters became as much an article topic as the answers themselves. One reporter for the *Times* in the United Kingdom wrote that when she did not like a question, which happened frequently, "she might sigh, tut dismissively or ignore it completely, leaving the terrible silence hanging until I move on."[45]

Staying Low Maintenance

Despite her increasing fame, Lavigne stuck with her low-maintenance look, even when she was traveling. Her beauty

Even after becoming famous, Lavigne kept her casual appearance.

routine centered on eye makeup, lip balm, and black nail polish. She had retired the neckties, noting that it was strange to go out in public and see so many people copying her. But she still kept her overall tomboy style, favoring camouflage prints.

Lavigne continued to ignore those who offered advice about her appearance. She often wore the same clothes over and over again, making a point of not sporting a new outfit for every occasion. Most people, she felt, had relatively few clothes to

Sardinia

Lavigne traveled a lot during her first tour, visiting many places around the world. One of her favorite spots was Sardinia, an island in the Mediterranean Sea that is part of Italy. Sardinia has scenic beaches, rugged mountains, and interesting caves as well as archaeological ruins.

"Sardinia's Emerald Coast has long been a favorite of crowned heads, movie stars and millionaires," according to In Italy Online. But Lavigne liked Sardinia's cuisine even better than the scenery. She raved about the local food, particularly the mozzarella cheese with tomatoes.

Quoted in "Welcome to Sardinia," In Italy Online, 2006. www.InItaly.com/regions/sardinia/sardinia.htm.

Sardinia is one of Lavigne's favorite places in the world.

choose from when they got dressed each day. "That's normal," she says. "I try to stay that way as much as I can."[46]

"Try to Shut Me Up"

One piece of normalcy Lavigne missed was sleeping in the same bed every night, something she had not been able to do during her overseas performances. Then, for the North American leg of her tour in April and May, Lavigne and her band chartered a tour bus equipped with bunk beds. Lavigne excitedly claimed the middle bunk for her first real road tour. Now she had a bit more of the stability she craved.

Though she enjoyed being on tour, Lavigne frequently missed the stability of home.

For the North American tour, billed as "Try to Shut Me Up," Lavigne's management, Nettwerk, purposely limited the number of concerts to prevent her from burning out. They also planned for her to visit each city only once, instead of multiple times. In describing their marketing strategy, her manager, Terry McBride, called this tour a "taste." He explained, "I want to leave the major touring [until] after she has a second album."[47]

Because "Try to Shut Me Up" was Lavigne's first extended tour in North America as the main or "headlining" act, her ability to draw big crowds there was unknown. Her manager's decision to arrange for Lavigne to play in large arenas such as the Air Canada Center in Toronto and Nassau Coliseum in Uniondale, New York, was therefore risky. She supplemented her *Let Go* material with some cover songs—her own versions of previously recorded songs, such as Green Day's "Basket Case"—to create a show about an hour long.

Compared to other promotional efforts, going on a road tour suited Lavigne, who had said consistently that performing onstage was her favorite part of being a singer. Now she had the chance to do it night after night. This tour was a special experience for all of the band members, too. Drummer Matt Brann says, "There definitely is nothing like your first big world tour. So few musicians ever get the chance to do what we did and I'll never forget it. Everything is just so new and exciting. Not that our . . . future tours won't be, there's just something really special about the innocence and sense of adventure that you have the first time around."[48]

Lavigne and her band soon proved they could hold their own as a headlining act. In April 2003 they played a sold-out show at the Corel Centre, where only four years before Lavigne had sung onstage with Shania Twain.

Mixed Concert Reviews

Overall, Lavigne's concerts received mixed reviews. The fact that she never lip-synched became apparent during the occasional missed notes, but in general, reviewers complimented her voice. MTV found her capable on the guitar, and some members of the press praised Lavigne for focusing on her music instead of relying on stage gimmicks and wardrobe changes to create a show.

The common negative theme in her reviews was that she lacked onstage energy. A reviewer for the *New York Times* even called her "a fake rock star" and said her only dance "consists of jumping up and down."[49] Some other critics agreed that she barely moved around on the stage.

Regardless of the negative press, Lavigne was still a big hit with her fans, many of whom were attending their first concerts. While the everyday clothes she wore onstage made her seem like one of her young fans, her voice was something that both parents and kids could enjoy.

Charitable Contributions

In between concert events, Lavigne used her fame to raise money for charity. For example, she recorded Bob Dylan's "Knockin' on Heaven's Door" to raise money for War Child Canada, an organization that helps children in war-affected areas. War Child provided funding to children's hospitals in Iraq, for instance, and bought textbooks for schools in war-torn countries. War Child included Lavigne's recording of the Dylan song on its *Peace Songs* CD. The compilation, which was released in April 2003, also included performance by artists such as David Bowie, Michelle Branch, and Barenaked Ladies. By May, the CD had raised $100,000.

In addition, Lavigne donated items to charity auctions for worthy causes. Her handwritten lyrics to "I'm with You," for example, were auctioned, along with autographed lyrics from other artists, to raise money for a cancer research and treatment center in Los Angeles.

Lavigne also helped a cause closer to home. An outbreak of SARS (severe acute respiratory syndrome) in Toronto negatively affected Canada's tourist industry after the World Health Organization issued a travel warning in April 2003. The city lost hundreds of millions of dollars from the dramatic decrease in tourism. To raise money for SARS-related charities and to help encourage visitors, Lavigne and many other musicians performed at a large benefit concert in Toronto in the summer of 2003. The event turned into one of the largest outdoor concerts ever held in North America, drawing an estimated 450,000 people.

Lavigne enjoyed playing for large crowds, but she quickly learned that stardom has a downside: Privacy in her personal life was now nearly impossible. When she took her "Try to Shut Me Up" tour to Australia, she found that she was unable to escape the press, even during vacation. While she was on a brief tour break, photographers spotted her at a beach with guitarist Jesse Colburn and managed to get a shot of the two musicians embracing by the water's edge. Lavigne denied any romantic relationship with Colburn, although it was widely believed that they were dating.

Songwriting with Evan Taubenfeld

Lavigne did not deny her songwriting relationship with her other guitarist, Evan Taubenfeld, who became part of getting the second CD underway. Lavigne had started writing tunes

Lavigne promotes her first CD during an interview at a radio station. In 2003 she began work on her follow-up album.

with him even before *Let Go* had been released the year before. They created a song together called "Don't Tell Me," and they continued to write new material on their days off from the "Try to Shut Me Up" tour. Lavigne and Taubenfeld created many new songs, but none were recorded due to their hectic performing schedule.

Then the tour, which grossed $9 million in the United States alone, came to an end in June 2003. Rather than take a break from music, Lavigne was energized to work on new material. She predicted that the music on her next CD would be less pop and more rock than her first CD, with more personal lyrics. Working with new people and more rock-oriented producers were also her goals.

She continued working with Taubenfeld, and after the tour ended, he and Lavigne wrote together in their Toronto hotel rooms. Lavigne commented on how much fun it was to create songs in her pajamas and skip showering if she wanted: "I don't have to look decent . . . face any cameras. . . . It's great."[50]

She and Taubenfeld were free to create music on their own schedule. Three of the songs they wrote would appear on her next CD: "Don't Tell Me," "Take Me Away," and "Freak Out." Her drummer, Matt Brann, also contributed to "Freak Out." So without even telling her record company, Lavigne had her second CD underway.

Chapter Four

Avril's Evolution

As Avril Lavigne began to work on her second CD in 2003, she knew from the start that the process would be different from that of the first one. There would be no need to work only with Arista-selected songwriting partners, no trying to ignore her country-pop audition, and no fearing that Arista would drop her if she did not come up with a good song quickly. With the success of her first album to back her up, she had the freedom to write with whomever she wanted.

Connecting with Chantal

Besides guitarist Evan Taubenfeld, Lavigne found another songwriting partner in Chantal Kreviazuk, a Canadian singer, songwriter, and classically trained pianist. Kreviazuk, who was a decade older than Lavigne, became part big sister, part inspiration, and new best friend.

After hitting it off over a lunch date in June 2003, Lavigne and Kreviazuk decided to write a song together. One session soon grew into two weeks of writing in partnership. Creating songs this way was an enjoyable experience because the two felt they could be open and honest with each other. When she compared it to the songwriting sessions Arista had set up for the first album, Lavigne said about working with her friend, "I can put out all my ideas . . . I don't hold anything back."[51] Kreviazuk, in turn, praised Lavigne's musical instincts and her ability to make decisions based on gut feelings.

Canadian singer Chantal Kreviazuk and Lavigne worked well together as songwriters for Lavigne's second CD.

The pair followed their initial spurt of songwriting with many more months of collaboration. After they had created twelve songs together in Toronto, Kreviazuk invited Lavigne to stay with her and her husband, Raine Maida, at their Malibu, California, home. Lavigne was familiar with Maida and his music because during the European leg of her tour earlier in 2003, his band, Our Lady Peace, had opened for her shows.

It came as a pleasant surprise to Lavigne that Maida was also a producer with a home studio. She ended up staying with Kreviazuk and Maida for about seven months. During that time, Maida worked with her to produce five of the songs she had written with his wife. In addition, he and Lavigne wrote another song, "Fall to Pieces," together. It was a fun and happy time for the singer, who laughingly recalls recording vocals in her pajamas.

Working with Ben Moody

In addition to working with Maida, Lavigne collaborated with two other producers: Don Gilmore, a producer for the bands Good Charlotte and Linkin Park, and Butch Walker from Marvelous 3. They each produced several songs for her second CD.

Gilmore, in turn, introduced Lavigne to Ben Moody, the former guitarist from the band Evanescence. Lavigne and Moody quickly became good friends. Their camaraderie resulted in work on a new song, "Nobody's Home," which Gilmore also produced.

An Encouraging Friend

In October 2003 Ben Moody abruptly left his band, Evanescence, after nearly a decade together. One of his next musical projects after the painful break was working with Lavigne on "Nobody's Home," which went on to become a top-ten hit.

Musically, Lavigne and Moody worked well together. Lavigne was also a good friend to him, which became evident in a later MTV interview. Moody spoke about being diagnosed with bipolar disorder and receiving treatment, and he talked about the role Lavigne played in encouraging him to pursue a solo career. Previously, Moody had not given much thought to creating an album of his own. But after he played one of his songs for Lavigne, she convinced him to try. "You're going to do a record, and that's that!" she said. The song he played for her, "Everything Burns," became the first single from the *Fantastic Four* movie soundtrack.

Quoted in Rodrigo Perez, "Ex-Evanescence Guitarist Ben Moody Thanks Avril for His Solo Career," MTV.com, July 14, 2005. www.MTV.com/news/articles/1505754/20050714/story.jhtml.

Personal Lyrics

Although "Nobody's Home" did not come from her own experience, many of Lavigne's other new songs were based on her life. For example, she wrote "Slipped Away" about her grandfather, who had died while she was on tour. Overall, she felt her lyrics were more personal on this CD than on the first one. "I feel like I'm handing out pages of my diary about me,"[52] she said.

The intimacy conveyed on this CD was intentional. With this recording, she wanted to share her thoughts and feelings, so she came up with the title *Under My Skin* to reflect the personal nature of the CD. "Lyrically, I was able to take [the CD] somewhere a little deeper and just express myself better,"[53] she says.

Leaving Out the Matrix

In creating *Under My Skin* in 2003 and early 2004, Lavigne decided not to work with the Matrix again. Given the success of the songs they created together for *Let Go*, such a decision might have surprised many in the music business. But after some members of the Matrix had brought her songwriting involvement into question, Lavigne did not want to repeat that experience. She used the second CD as a testament to her songwriting and hoped to put to rest any doubts about her abilities. During the making and release of *Under My Skin*, she did not even want to talk about the Matrix during interviews.

Another consideration was that Lavigne had altered her musical style over the past two years, and she wanted *Under My Skin* to reflect that change. Lavigne did concede that as much as she wanted more rock songs on this album than on *Let Go*, there needed to be some pop tunes if the CD was to receive widespread radio play. Her goal, she said, was to include "catchy ones, but not cheesy pop like some songs off the last record."[54]

Indeed, Lavigne felt she had matured since beginning work on her first CD at age sixteen. "I'm a lot wiser now,"[55] she said in 2003 after turning nineteen. For example, she felt more knowledgeable about the business side of the music industry. She had also become more adept at dealing with her record label's employees. Rather than letting them review each song as she

Lavigne promotes her second CD, **Under My Skin,** *in Australia in 2004.*

recorded it, she was able to convince them to let her create at her own pace. Since Lavigne had proven that she could deliver, the record company let her work without much interference.

Award Losses

Lavigne's maturing as an artist was not, however, rewarded at the Grammys in February 2004. She was nominated for Best Female Pop Vocal Performance ("I'm with You"), Song of the Year ("I'm With You"), and Best Female Rock Vocal Performance ("Losing Grip"). After losing in 2003, she approached the awards in 2004 with a different attitude, saying that while it was an honor, the nomination was "nothing you want to take

My World

In November 2003 Lavigne released a DVD/CD set called *My World*. The CD gave fans a chance to hear "Why," the song she wrote with Peter Zizzo that had helped secure her Arista contract. The CD also included live versions of "Unwanted" and "Sk8er Boi," along with covers, her own versions of previously recorded songs, which she performed during various concerts.

The DVD contained footage from an hour-long concert she performed in Buffalo, New York, during her "Try to Shut Me Up" tour. It also featured several music videos and forty minutes of behind-the-scenes footage from the tour. Some of the fun moments recorded include Lavigne skateboarding and taking an occasional spill, along with her getting locked in the bathroom on a chartered private jet. *My World* became one of the top five best-selling music DVDs in 2003.

Lavigne greets fans at the screening of her My World *DVD in 2003.*

too seriously."[56] In the end, although she admitted that she would like to win, Lavigne walked away empty-handed again.

She did not fare better at the Junos, either. A DVD documenting part of her first tour, *My World*, was nominated for Music DVD of the Year but lost. She also lost the Fan Choice Award, which went to the Canadian group Nickelback. Her losses put her in good company, though. Sum 41 and Our Lady Peace failed to win a 2004 Juno as well.

Despite the losses, Lavigne was still someone that people saw in a positive light. In April, *Teen People* numbered her among its "20 Teens Who Will Change the World" for her work with War Child Canada. "I hope my involvement will pique people's interest in this cause,"[57] she said. Because of her position as a role model for other teenagers, she wanted to learn what she could about the situations in war-affected countries. She felt she could take advantage of her fame to teach other kids and increase awareness about some of the world's problems.

Settling Down

When Lavigne was not promoting her favorite charity or her music, she could often be found relaxing at her new home. She had bought a three-story attached house in Toronto and moved out of her family's Napanee residence in March 2004. She was pleased to have settled down and be on her own, stating, "It's good to be . . . doing normal things. I love to cook, and I love to clean."[58] Above all, she seemed to enjoy the sense of normalcy and stability that having her own home gave her.

Other parts of Lavigne's life were also becoming stable, as she settled into a relationship with Deryck Whibley. Lavigne had laughingly told *Teen People* that they were friends. Although she was never one to talk much about her love life, photographs of the couple appeared in the press, giving credence to the stories that the two were involved with each other.

Changes

As much as Lavigne's personal life was steady, she faced other challenges over which she had little control. In March 2004 Jesse

By 2004 Lavigne had happily settled into a relationship with Deryck Whibley of Sum 41.

Colburn left the band and was replaced by Craig Wood, the bassist for the group Gob. Gob had been an opening act during her first tour, so she was familiar with Wood's guitar playing.

Perhaps of greater significance for Lavigne's career was L.A. Reid's departure from Arista earlier in 2004. Lavigne denied any real disruption, however. As she prepared to market her new album, she said her managers buffered her from the personnel changes at Arista, and that they were "making sure it doesn't have an effect on me."[59]

Live and by Surprise

Reid's departure from Arista did not seem to change Lavigne's basic relationship with the label: She had a new CD and Arista needed her to promote it. To publicize her latest album, she scheduled shows at more than twenty shopping centers starting in March 2004 and ending in mid-April. She and Taubenfeld would offer acoustic guitar performances in malls across the United States and in several Canadian cities. They named the mini-tour "Avril Live and by Surprise," since the exact concert

In 2004 Lavigne and Evan Taubenfeld went on a mall tour to promote her second CD. Here they perform at a shopping center in Ohio.

location for each show was announced only two days in advance by her online fan club and local radio stations.

Mall concerts were considered unusual for a singer with Lavigne's level of fame, since she was capable of drawing sellout crowds to large arenas. The point of this mini-tour, however, was to get her new music out to young fans quickly. Each free show lasted about a half hour and featured several songs from her new CD along with a few of her well-known hits.

For her mall tour, Lavigne sported a new look. Her hair, while still straight, was now a bleached color with black sections. She said of her style, "It's not, like, Gucci. Not high-end [stuff]. Grungy but glam."[60] Taubenfeld, whose hair was blond, sported black streaks, too.

Feuding with Hilary Duff

Lavigne's promotion of her new album showed a maturing business sense, but she still had not grown out of creating controversy. While she was speaking live on a Boston radio station in March 2004, she responded to comments made previously by Hilary Duff, another teen singer. Duff had disapproved of Lavigne's annoyance at fans who imitated her style of dress. Lavigne denied ever treating her fans badly, saying, "I think it's a compliment that my fans dress like me." Then she called Duff, who was not there at the time, a "goody-two shoes."[61] During a later interview with *Newsweek*, Lavigne criticized Duff for not writing her own songs.

Duff soon sought to end the feud. In April her representative told *People* magazine that Duff was a fan of Lavigne's music, and that her comment had been "blown out of proportion."[62] When learning of this later, Lavigne accepted the peace offering, and their feud ended.

Being Stalked

The spat with Duff was a distraction, but of greater concern to Lavigne and her family was a stalking incident that ultimately resulted in the arrest of an obsessive fan. James Speedy, a thirty-

In 2004 Hilary Duff (pictured) accused Lavigne of being annoyed with her fans.

year-old man from Lynnwood, Washington, had been sending the Lavignes e-mails, gifts such as flowers and wine, and letters for some time. The letters were more annoying than threatening, but her family became concerned when Speedy wrote to them saying that he would be visiting Napanee. The Lavignes informed the local police of the situation, and in July 2003 Speedy was arrested when the police found him sitting in a car parked across from the Lavignes' family home. He told the Ontario Provincial Police that he came to Napanee "to be part of her family."[63] The police released him, but he was forbidden from contacting Lavigne and her family again. In addition, he was told he could not return to Canada for one year.

Canadian police officials notified their counterparts in Lynnwood of Speedy's activities. Although Speedy's communications were not hostile, the *Seattle Times* reported that police in

A Complicated Song

As *Let Go* continued to achieve commercial success, Lavigne's music also became a target of parody. In 2003 "Weird Al" Yankovic, known for his spoofs of famous songs, released a new album, *Poodle Hat*. His version of "Complicated," called "A Complicated Song," included humorous lyrics such as, "Tell me, why'd you have to go and make me so constipated."

He also created a mock interview with Lavigne, where he spliced clips from her previously taped interviews to make it seem like she was responding to his questions. The resulting video made Lavigne seem ditzy and confused. Although the video was not altogether flattering, the hilarious song was a sure sign that she had become a pop culture icon.

"Weird Al" Yankovic parodied Lavigne's song "Complicated."

Lynnwood and Ontario said Lavigne and her family "felt uneasy over his attention."[64]

The unwanted attention continued, however. That spring, after Speedy learned that Lavigne would be playing at a mall in the Seattle area, he contacted her management about attending the concert. This worried Lavigne and her family, and the police were notified. Speedy was arrested for stalking the day of her performance in Seattle. Police subsequently searched his home and found three guns, as well as letters to Lavigne. He was eventually convicted of stalking, with reduced charges resulting in a month of jail time and no contact with the singer or her parents for two years.

Disliking "Complicated"

With the stalking threat resolved with the arrest, Lavigne's tour proceeded uneventfully. Some observers even thought she seemed bored during her performances. A reporter for MTV noted that Lavigne's zest for playing live appeared limited to her new songs, while singing "Complicated" and "Sk8er Boi" seemed like a chore for her. Lavigne agreed that she was losing her enthusiasm for some of her songs. "I can't stand performing 'Complicated,'"[65] she admitted during an interview with *Rolling Stone*.

She said she would continue to perform the song, however, because it was a fan favorite. She did not always sing it with the original lyrics, though. During her European tour, she took a cue from a parody Weird Al Yankovic had written and sang, "Why do I feel so constipated?"[66] during a United Kingdom performance.

Total Request Live

When *Under My Skin* hit the stores in May 2004, it gave Lavigne a chance to focus more on her current songs than her old ones. She made the publicity rounds for her album, including a live concert broadcast over the Internet and various television appearances.

It was during one such appearance that she continued her controversial attitude toward the press. While she was on MTV's *Total Request Live* in May, host Damien Fahey questioned her

Lavigne's **Under My Skin** *CD did not sell as many copies as her debut, but still climbed to the top of the* **Billboard** *charts.*

about her relations with the media. In response, she stuck up her middle finger toward the camera. She later said she was just kidding around about how annoying the press was, but she recognized that she had appeared angry instead. For its part, MTV cut short her scheduled segment on the show and did not allow her to continue her performance as planned.

Songwriting Revisited

Despite her misstep on *TRL*, Lavigne continued with other promotions. It was important that *Under My Skin* do well commercially. Otherwise, Lavigne risked being labeled a one-album wonder. Lavigne denied feeling the pressure, saying she would be happy whether her second CD sold millions of copies or not. But there was more than sales and income at stake. Lavigne's credibility as a songwriter was also riding on this album. Unlike *Let Go*, which did not include writing credits, *Under My Skin* listed every song as having been written by Avril Lavigne or written by Avril Lavigne and a cowriter.

Early indications were not particularly encouraging. The first released track, "Don't Tell Me," had been available for radio play since March 2004. Despite the song's positive girl-power message about abstinence, the stations were not playing it as much as they had played her songs from *Let Go*. Overall, music critics complimented her voice and delivery on *Under My Skin*, and praised the production. But some of her lyrics, which she had intended to carry deeper meaning, were criticized by reviewers as self-obsessed.

Fans seemed to appreciate what the critics did not, however. Regardless of the disappointing radio play of "Don't Tell Me," *Under My Skin* still hit the number-one spot on *Billboard* album charts in June 2004. Next, Arista released the second single "My Happy Ending," which fared better both in sales and on the charts than "Don't Tell Me." Although *Under My Skin* did not sell as many copies as *Let Go*, it too eventually went multiplatinum.

Life Outside of Music

For her part, Lavigne indicated that she was happy with the way her career was going. On MuchMusic's show *Intimate and Interactive*, she expressed how content she was. When someone asked her about becoming famous so quickly, she noted, "To deal with that [celebrity] happening to you, you have to have a good head on your shoulders and be thankful and not think of yourself as some great thing."[67]

Lavigne tried to behave as though her chosen career was like any other. For example, she avoided being chauffeured in limousines, preferring a less ostentatious SUV. She rejected offers to endorse consumer products, saying she preferred to sell her music instead.

Lavigne also made a point of enjoying time with her family, including her younger sister, Michelle. When they were able to be together, they would focus on typical teenage girl activities like trying on clothes and experimenting with hairstyles and makeup. "We just do normal sister stuff,"[68] Lavigne says.

Denying Engagement Rumors

Still, trying to live a normal life while being an object of scrutiny by the press was difficult at best. The attention surrounding Lavigne's relationship with Whibley was typical of her dealings with the media. In September 2004 a London tabloid reported that Whibley had proposed to Lavigne, getting down on one knee before giving her a ring. What actually transpired was unclear. Lavigne and Whibley may have staged such a pose to mislead the celebrity-chasing photographers known as paparazzi.

Sum 41's representatives denied the rumors, and Lavigne's publicity people refused to comment one way or another. Lavigne, however, wore a ring to the World Music Awards rehearsals on the Monday after the supposed engagement took place. Even though this supported the proposal story, rumors about an engagement turned out to be false. Although Lavigne and Whibley were not making wedding plans, she did have a new tattoo on her wrist: the letter "D" inside a red outline of a heart.

Even as rumors circulated about her personal life, Lavigne prepared for her second tour in the fall of 2004. She named the tour "Bonez," playing off the title of her CD, *Under My Skin*. She was ready to perform live in venues around the world, and she would also embark on some nonmusical adventures as well.

Chapter Five

Sustaining Success

Avril Lavigne promoted *Under My Skin* by touring for many months during 2004 and 2005, but that did not stop her from expanding into other artistic ventures. She landed three small movie roles and expressed a newfound interest in fashion and modeling. With her existing success in the music industry and her diverse new projects, Lavigne seemed poised to sustain her career over the long run.

Taubenfeld Moves On

Lavigne worked hard to ensure the success of *Under My Skin*, and touring was a big part of her promotional efforts. In September 2004 Lavigne began her worldwide "Bonez" tour, with one major change: Lead guitarist and cowriter Evan Taubenfeld decided to leave the band and pursue his own musical career. What he really wanted to do was sing his own songs, with his own group, he says. "With Avril, I wasn't doing what I loved,"[69] he explained about his decision to strike out on his own. Taubenfeld started his own group, Hate Me, and got a record deal with Sire Records/Warner Brothers. They began recording their first album in 2006.

Lavigne's comments suggested that she had accepted Taubenfeld's need to work on other musical projects. "[Evan and I] have been good friends since he joined the band, and it's sad for me to see him go, and at the same time, I wish him luck. . . . I think

In 2004 Evan Taubenfeld left Lavigne's band to pursue his own musical career.

Evan is talented. I think he's a great guy and he deserves the best,"[70] she says.

Beginning the "Bonez" Tour

Devin Bronson replaced Taubenfeld. Along with her new guitarist and other band members, Lavigne performed in Europe in late September through mid-October 2004, then headed to the United States and Canada to put on shows through the end of November.

The tour's promoters felt that Lavigne was able to cross over to a more diverse audience with her second album. The variety of radio stations that were playing her songs from *Under My Skin* supported this point. Although kids still loved her music, many adults had become fans, too.

Concert planners in the United States knew that this was still a show that many younger fans would attend with their parents, however, and that affected their marketing efforts. They wanted to reach mothers as well as their daughters, so they used newspaper advertisements along with the typical radio promotions to get the word out. Concert planners hoped the relatively inexpensive price of tickets (under forty dollars) would encourage families or groups of moms and kids to attend.

The concerts themselves were different on this tour, too. Although Lavigne still skipped the costume changes and troupes of backup dancers used by some teenage female performers, the concert staging on this tour was more complex than her first. For example, the lighting effects and other production details were more elaborate. This tour required five trucks to transport the stage equipment and paraphernalia, while the first concert required only two.

New Musical Skills

Another element that made the "Bonez" concerts different from her previous ones was that Lavigne branched out and demonstrated her skills with various instruments. For instance, she played drums on a cover song, letting her producer and opening act Butch Walker handle the vocals. Kreviazuk had taught her the piano for the songs they wrote together, so Lavigne played that instrument on tour, too. She also continued to use her guitar, and did several acoustic songs alone. "I feel like I've stepped up a notch performing,"[71] she says.

Despite the changes in her concerts, not everyone agreed. Some of those who reviewed her performances offered the same criticisms that had been aimed at her in the past. They felt that during her performances, she still did not connect with her fans and create a stage presence. She barely spoke to her audience or

Lavigne performs for fans at an outdoor concert in Toronto, Canada. In 2005 she was nominated for five Juno Awards, Canada's equivalent to the Grammys.

her band members. "Avril's stage patter is as canned and dull as her music,"[72] one critic says.

Other reviewers, however, complimented her guitar and piano playing, as well as her improved stage presence. She also received praise for her happy energy during the concerts, exemplified by how she smiled and skipped around the stage during her shows. By the end of the tour, Lavigne herself felt that she had learned to interact with the crowd more and thought her performance had improved overall.

Anti-Lip-Synching

Like the previous tours, "Bonez" involved lots of hard work, but Lavigne was unwilling to resort to such tactics as lip-synching, even though prerecorded vocals would have guaranteed a uniform sound at each performance. Another young singer, Ashlee Simpson, had faced ridicule after she was revealed to be lip-synching during an appearance on *Saturday Night Live* in October 2004. On the live show, Simpson's voice could be heard, but she was not even holding a microphone.

Lavigne had never made a secret of her disdain for lip-synching. After the Ashlee Simpson fiasco, she became even more vocal in her opinions. She commented to an MTV reporter that lip-synching was "a disgrace to the music industry."[73] Lavigne felt strongly that performing live was a big part of being a singer.

Avril in the News

Whether it was her outspokenness over lip-synching or other news items, Lavigne found herself making headlines in 2004. This trend continued in 2005, in part due to her charitable efforts. In January she played in a Vancouver concert for tsunami relief. Lavigne performed along with her boyfriend in Sum 41, Chantal Kreviazuk, and Raine Maida, as well as other Canadian singers. The benefit raised almost $3 million to help victims of the tsunami that devastated Indonesia, Sri Lanka, and other areas on December 26, 2004.

Another way in which Lavigne made news was with the 2005 Juno Awards. Although she did not receive any Grammy nominations, she received five Juno nominations for her work on *Under My Skin*. Her touring schedule in Asia caused her to miss the actual awards ceremony in Canada, but her absence did not stop her from triumphing. She won Artist of the Year, Pop Album of the Year, and the Fan Choice Award at the April 2005 ceremony.

After touring in Asia, Lavigne performed in Australia, then flew to a show in Johannesburg, South Africa. It was her first visit to Africa, and she had a huge turnout for the event. Almost twenty thousand fans, some as young as five years old, came to hear her sing.

Hamming It Up

Her worldwide tour schedule may have been grueling, but Lavigne seemed energized by performing and appeared to need little downtime. When she did take brief breaks, the paparazzi hounded her. Lavigne felt the press could exaggerate a simple night out with friends into a severe drinking problem. She did admit to hamming it up for the photographers because of her lack of respect for tabloid magazines. For example, even though she was not a smoker, she would hold a cigarette when she knew the photographers were snapping away.

The reality was quite different from what the tabloids portrayed. Not only did she not smoke at all, but she rarely drank. Instead, she was eating a mostly vegan diet and doing yoga, hallmarks of someone practicing a healthy lifestyle. "I'm completely opposite of what everyone thinks I am right now,"[74] she says.

Still, not everything the tabloids printed was false. Whibley and Lavigne had bought a new home together in California, so when rumors swirled that the two had gotten engaged in June 2005, the tabloids had a field day. This time, the stories were true. Whibley had proposed while Lavigne was on tour in Europe. She accepted and he gave her a five-carat diamond engagement ring while the pair was in Venice, Italy.

Image Changes

As Lavigne's status changed from committed dating to engaged, her image began to change as well. She was maturing, and it showed. During a North American tour in July and August, she started performing in flowing skirts instead of the pants and T-shirts she usually wore on tour. She did skip the high heels, however, opting for a pair of comfortable sneakers instead. Her

Matthew Brann

As Lavigne's guitarists have changed over the years, drummer Matthew Brann remains as the only original band member. When Brann is not touring with Lavigne, he writes music with other artists. But music is not the only thing keeping Brann busy. He is also interested in supporting autism awareness through the Durham chapter of Autism Society Ontario. He became involved through an autistic boy in his parents' neighborhood. He explains, "I have been very lucky and fortunate in life so I thought that if I could lend some support to a good cause and try to help raise some awareness then why not! I keep in touch with members of the Durham chapter and try to chip in whenever I can." Donating items for fundraising auctions, attending events, and displaying the organization's logo on his drums during a concert are some of the ways that Brann has assisted.

Matthew Brann, e-mail interview by author, March 21, 2006

hair was curlier and blonder. Lavigne says about her new look, "That's what girls do. When they grow up, they start wearing makeup and dresses."[75]

While discussing how she had changed, Lavigne describes herself in *Cosmopolitan* magazine as more feminine, particularly "the amount of time it takes me to get ready . . . and how much I like shopping and clothes now."[76] She was clearly having fun in the process of leaving behind her tomboy image.

Punk'd

One event caught on camera may not have been as fun for Lavigne. In August MTV aired an episode of *Punk'd*, a show in which prankster Ashton Kutcher sets a celebrity up for an elaborate joke, in this case featuring Lavigne. In this prank, Chantal Kreviazuk served as an accomplice, persuading Lavigne to pull her car into a specific spot in a parking garage. When they left the

Lavigne and Usher appeared on the cover of the November 2005 issue of Teen Vogue.

car, Kutcher had a "Reserved" sign installed and had another driver park behind Lavigne's car. When Lavigne and Kreviazuk returned, the driver told them they would have to wait for her to finish working before she would move the car, since Lavigne had parked in her space.

Sum 41 and the Congo

Lavigne became engaged to boyfriend Deryck Whibley in June 2005. Whibley is the lead singer and guitarist for the Canadian band Sum 41. The band was formed in 1996 when Whibley and members of rival bands created a new group forty-one days into that summer.

Like Lavigne, Sum 41 has been supportive of War Child Canada. As part of their efforts, members of Sum 41 agreed to film their trip to the Democratic Republic of Congo in May 2004 to educate others on the effects of war. The humanitarian trip was interrupted after five days when shooting erupted nearby. Fearing for their safety, United Nations employee Chuck Pelletier evacuated the band amid gunfire. Their escape was captured in the resulting documentary, *Rocked: Sum 41 in Congo*. Out of gratitude to the man who rescued them, Sum 41 named their next album *Chuck*.

In 2004, Sum 41's visit to the Congo was cut short when violence erupted.

The woman walked away, leaving Lavigne's car blocked in. Then as part of the prank, a man showed up and offered to help steer the car while Lavigne pushed. As Kutcher had planned, the car rolled into a transformer and a motorcycle. The transformer caught fire and the car and motorcycle were damaged. When more people arrived at the scene, someone asked if she had helped move the car. Lavigne denied doing so—which clearly was not true. The incident could have portrayed her badly, but fortunately for Lavigne, the cameras recorded her wanting to call the police, and captured her relief that no one had been injured in what she still thought was a genuine accident.

Kutcher had portrayed Lavigne as a tough girl before the prank. But the anger and harshness he may have expected never surfaced. Lavigne became teary and emotional upon learning she had been "punk'd."

Taking Time for Herself

Lavigne was, in fact, plenty tough, as evidenced by her ability to adhere to a rigorous schedule touring around the world practically nonstop through September 2005. Over the summer of 2005 alone, she performed thirty-five shows.

But Lavigne knew the importance of not being consumed by her work. "You can't put your career before your life,"[77] she says. She wanted to continue creating fresh material and be careful of not burning out. She cited Green Day and Madonna as artists who were able to reinvent themselves and continue their careers over the long term.

Lavigne finished the last leg of her tour in South America during September 2005. Then she planned on taking a break from the music business and spending time "with my little sweetheart [Deryck],"[78] before working on her third album.

From Music to Movies

Although wrapping up her tour meant a musical hiatus for Lavigne, she had new projects to tackle. She had her first movie experience earlier in 2005 when she provided the voice for an

Lavigne and actors Nick Nolte and Bruce Willis celebrate the screening of Over the Hedge *at the Cannes Film Festival in 2006.*

opossum named Heather in the animated movie *Over the Hedge*. Then she received a small role in a movie called *The Flock*, starring Richard Gere and Claire Danes. Lavigne said she wanted to try acting on the big screen by starting with a small role, to "see how I like it and make sure I'm comfortable."[79] In this film, a police officer, played by Gere, wants to interview a man, and Lavigne plays the man's girlfriend. Sporting a chipped tooth and glasses for the part, she filmed her scenes in New Mexico at the end of November 2005.

Lavigne also signed on for a role as a restaurant worker in the movie *Fast Food Nation*. The movie was based on the nonfiction book, *Fast Food Nation: The Dark Side of the All-American Meal*, which showed the evils of the fast food industry. Richard Linklater, director of *School of Rock*, would direct. Even though the

Lavigne and her fellow actors pause to take direction while filming a scene for **Fast Food Nation.**

book was nonfiction, the movie would not be a documentary. Linklater planned to approach it by creating characters to illustrate the facts in the book. The movie was scheduled for a 2006 release.

Lavigne seemed to enjoy her foray into acting. "It's been a very busy and exciting past few months for me," she said about her film roles in an online letter to her fans. "Having the opportunity to act has been amazing and a lot fun."[80]

Fashionable Changes

Along with acting, Lavigne displayed a newfound interest in fashion. She signed with the Ford Modeling Agency at the end of 2005, and in February 2006, *Harper's Bazaar* included a fashion spread with Lavigne modeling four-thousand-dollar dresses.

The black streaked hair and chipped nail polish were long gone as she showed off an elegant hairdo and French manicured nails in the glamorous photos. In the accompanying *Harper's* article, Lavigne expressed an interest in modeling expensive products. Earlier in the year, she had been spotted at a Chanel fashion show in Paris, followed by one at New York's Fashion Week.

Sharon Haver, founder of FocusOnStyle.com, felt Lavigne's new look showed her growth as a person. Lavigne, she says, was

> no longer a one-dimensional punk kid. She's a young woman and she's open to different style ideas. She started out having this very one-dimensional image, with the [tank top] and the tie. And that was really great. It created an instant impression in everyone's mind. When you thought of her, you thought of what she looked like and it was wonderful for branding that way and making her mark. But she's proved herself and now she can go and venture in different directions. . . . It's a part of growing up.[81]

Charitable Efforts

When Lavigne was not exploring the world of movies and fashion, she continued to provide support for charities. Along with twenty other international celebrities, she became involved in an HIV/AIDS public awareness campaign, sponsored by YouthAIDS and the shoe company ALDO. Her black-and-white photo appeared with her quote: "Be Strong, Stand Up, Make a Difference."[82]

In another effort to support charity, Lavigne used her music to raise money for Amnesty International, an organization that works to protect human rights. As part of an Amnesty fundraiser, she recorded John Lennon's song "Imagine." Chantal Kreviazuk accompanied her on the piano, and Butch Walker handled the production.

New Directions

Although Lavigne was busy supporting charities, she had certainly not forgotten her own career. In February 2006 she reunited with former bandmate Taubenfeld to sing at the closing ceremonies of the Olympic Winter Games in Torino, Italy. Her performance was part of an effort to promote the 2010 winter games, which are to be held in Vancouver, Canada.

She also had started writing new songs for her third album. In March she wrote a note for her Web site about her next musical efforts. She reassured fans that she still enjoyed her other hits, a point that she felt might have been misconstrued in a recent article: "I was asked about my direction for the next record and said it probably wouldn't be so much on the dark side. Not that I think my [previous] record was 'so dark,' but I was just trying to say I'm at a really happy place in my life and that will most likely reflect in my songwriting."[83]

Lavigne's happiness continued when she married Whibley on July 15, 2006. They wed in a traditional ceremony on a private estate in California, complete with a flower-covered awning and a pond with white swans. Lavigne wore a custom-made strapless ivory gown and carried white roses as her father walked her down the aisle. At the reception, Lavigne and Whibley's first dance was to "Iris," her favorite song by the Goo Goo Dolls. Butch Walker called the wedding "storybook beautiful."[84]

Long-Lasting Fan Appeal

As Lavigne's life continues to change, DJ Race Taylor predicts that the singer will display increased maturity in her next album. "She's without a doubt grown up and become more refined right in front of our eyes," he says. "You would think that would have to also be apparent in what happens to her musically."[85]

No matter what direction her music takes in the future, at least some observers predict that many of her fans will continue to support her. Sharifa Mohamed, Webmaster and owner of the fan site Avril Lavigne Bandaids, explains Lavigne's long-lasting appeal:

When she first hit the [music] scene, Avril made an impression as a relatable icon. She also had the songs and the writing ability to turn what could have been a short-lived media infatuation into genuine respect. Now three years later, after much maturation and image change, it's the music that keeps people interested. As a tie-wearing teenager, Avril

Concertgoers cheer and snap photos while Lavigne performs on stage. Many believe she will have fans for a long time to come.

taught fans it was okay to be different. Now as a young woman, she teaches fans it's okay to be normal.[86]

Patrick Schabe, the music reviews editor for PopMatters.com, thinks her normalcy is part of her appeal.

She's spunky and sort of devil-may-care in her media appearances, and if she's wrapped up in stardom and the pressures of fame, she manages to make it seem like she's not taking things overly serious," Schabe says. "At the same time, she does possess a solid voice. . .her voice and image

Lavigne has matured into a woman who is happy with her music and her life.

seem well-matched to make her seem sort of like a sweet little sister who's part tough girl and part fragile teenager.[87]

As that teenager has grown up, she seems content with the choices she has made. During one interview, when asked what she would change in her life, Lavigne responded with a smile, "I like this one . . . It's so totally perfect. I wouldn't change a thing."[88]

Introduction: A Star with Staying Power

1. Quoted in Heather McCoy, "Avril Clones Beware," *Saskatoon Star Phoenix*, January 7, 2006. www.canada.com/saskatoonstarphoenix/story.html?id=7bd7d6e7-4de4-4635-b506-b8f6cdcd78ac&k=69546.

Chapter 1: Preparing for Stardom

2. Quoted in VH1, "Driven—Avril Lavigne," episode 49, April 23, 2004.

3. Quoted in Chris Willman, "Avril Lavigne the Anti-Britney," *Entertainment Weekly*, November 1, 2002, p. 22.

4. Quoted in VH1, "Driven—Avril Lavigne."

5. Cornerstone Christian Academy, press release sent to author, October 11, 2005.

6. Quoted in Jenny Eliscu, "Little Miss Can't Be Wrong," *Rolling Stone*, March 20, 2003, p. 38.

7. Quoted in Shanda Deziel, "Avril's Edge," *MacLean's*, January 13, 2003, p. 23.

8. Quoted in Ann Marie McQueen, "Avril's Wild Ride to Stardom," *Ottawa Sun*, February 9, 2003.

9. Quoted in Paul Cantin, "The Real Lavigne," *Toronto Star*, August 17, 2002, p. H13.

10. Quoted in McQueen, "Avril's Wild Ride to Stardom."

11. Quoted in Stevie Lin Thacker, "And the Winner Is . . . Avril Lavigne," *Scholastic Scope*, April 25, 2003, p. 10.

12. Quoted in Edmund J. Lee, "What She Wants Is What She Gets," *New York Times*, November 24, 2002, p. 2.31.

13. Quoted in Eliscu, "Little Miss Can't Be Wrong."

Chapter 2: A Complicated CD

14. Quoted in McQueen, "Avril's Wild Ride to Stardom."

15. Quoted in Larry LeBlanc, "Lavigne's Music Takes Hold With Arista's 'Let Go,'" *Billboard*, June 22, 2002, p. 14.

16. Quoted in Nekesa Mumbi Moody, "Invasion of the Anti-Britneys," *Toronto Star*, July 27, 2002, p. H10.

17. Willman, "Avril Lavigne the Anti-Britney."

18. Quoted in Alicia Clott, "Avril Lavigne," *Girls' Life*, August/September 2002, p. 46.

19. Quoted in Norman Provencher, "The Lavigne Project," *Ottawa Citizen*, August 17, 2002, p. E3.

20. Matthew Brann, e-mail interview by author, March 21, 2006.

21. Quoted in MTV.com Media, "Avril Lavigne On Her Band," July 12, 2002. www.MTV.com.

22. Race Taylor, phone interview by author, March 24, 2006.

23. Quoted in *MuchMusic.com*, "Transcript: MuchOnDemand," April 17, 2002. www.muchmusic.com/music/artists/tran scripts.asp?artist=11&transcript=4.

24. Sharon Haver, phone interview by author, March 21, 2006.

25. Quoted in Jenny Eliscu, "Avril Lavigne," *Rolling Stone*, October 31, 2002, p. 118.

26. Cantin, "The Real Lavigne."

27. Quoted in Willman, "Avril Lavigne the Anti-Britney."

28. Quoted in Lorraine Ali, "Anarchy on MTV? Tough Gals, Rejoice," *Newsweek*, December 30, 2002–January 6, 2003, p. 79.

29. Quoted in Lauren David Peden, "Punk Rocker, Pop Queen, and Tomboy All in One," *New York Times*, November 10, 2002, p. ST1.

30. Quoted in "Driven—Avril Lavigne."

31. Quoted in Corey Moss, "Britney Spears, Avril Lavigne Fall into the Matrix," MTV.com, March 13, 2003. www.mtv.com/news/articles/1470503/20030313/story.jhtml.

32. Quoted in Eliscu, "Little Miss Can't Be Wrong."

33. Quoted in CTV.ca, "Two Canadians Win at the MTV Music Video Awards," August 30, 2002. www.ctv.ca/servlet/Arti cleNews/story/CTVNews/1030627753030_181.

34. Quoted in MuchMusic.com, "Transcript: MuchOnDemand."

Chapter 3: Balancing Fame and Normalcy

35. David Remington, phone interview by author, March 2, 2006.

36. Quoted in Edna Gunderson, "Grammys Come of Age, Both Young and Old," *USA Today*, February 21, 2003, p. 09D.

37. Abbey Goodman, "Durst Dresses for a Gray Mood, Avril Gets Hideous, Rappers Turn Pink on Grammy Red Carpet," MTV.com, February 23, 2003. www.mtv.com/news/arti cles/1470106/20030223/story.jhtml.

38. Remington, interview.

39. Quoted in Shirley Halperin, "All About Avril," *Us Weekly*, February 3, 2003, p. 74.

40. Quoted in Larry LeBlanc, "Arista's Lavigne Tops Juno Awards with Four Wins," *Billboard*, April 19, 2003, p. 7.

41. Ben Rayner, "The Avril & Shania Show," *Toronto Star*, April 7, 2003, p. B01.

42. Ann Marie McQueen, e-mail interview by author, February 8, 2006.

43. McQueen, interview.

44. Quoted in Deziel, "Avril's Edge."

45. Johnny Davis, "Angelic Upstart," the *Times* (London), September 18, 2004, p. 24.

46. Quoted in Daphne Gordon, "Childhood T's a Basic of Tomboy Style," *Toronto Star*, January 16, 2003, p. D03.

47. Quoted in Susanne Ault, "Lavigne Tour Intended as 'Just a Taste,'" *Billboard*, February, 1, 2003.

48. Brann, interview.

49. Kelefa Sanneh, "This Is for You, Mom and Dad," *New York Times*, April 12, 2003, p. D7.

50. Quoted in MTV.com, "No Showers, Just Songs," July 25, 2003. www.mtv.com/bands/l/lavigne_avril/news_feature_ 07_25_2003.

51. Quoted in Joe D'Angelo, "Avril Lavigne: No Looking Back," MTV.com, March 22, 2004. www.mtv.com/bands/l/lavigne _avril/news_feature_032204.

52. Quoted in Greg Kot, "Lavigne Seeks Maturity with 'Skin,'" *Chicago Tribune*, May 27, 2004, p. 3.

53. Quoted in MuchMusic.com, "Transcript: Intimate & Interactive," May 28, 2004. www.muchmusic.com/music/artists/ transcripts.asp?artist=11&transcript=2.

54. Quoted in *Entertainment Weekly*, "Music," Issue 747/748, January 23, 2004 –January 30, 2004.

55. Quoted in Joe D'Angelo, "Avril Lavigne Grows Up, Sheds Her Newbie Ways for Upcoming LP," MTV.com, November 6, 2003. www.mtv.com/news/articles/1480231/11062003/ lavigne_avril.jhtml.

56. Quoted in Brian Hiatt, "Northern Light," EW.com, January 28, 2004. www.ew.com/ew/report/0,6115,581367_4%7C 43996%7C%7C0_0_,00.html.

57. Quoted in Doreen Arriaga, "20 Teens Who Will Change the World," *Teen People*, April 2004, p. 124.

58. Quoted in D'Angelo, "Avril Lavigne: No Looking Back."

59. Quoted in Deborah Evans Price, "Avril Goes Back to Basics," *Billboard*, Volume 116, Issue 21, May 22, 2004.

60. Quoted in Craig McLean, "Riot Girl," the *Independent* (London), May 22, 2004, p. 12.

61. Quoted in Gayle Lee and Laura Raposa, "Avril Showers Rival with Trash Talk in Hub," *The Boston Herald*, March 17, 2004, p. 26.

62. Quoted in *People*, "Why Can't We All Just Get Along," April 5, 2004, p. 20.

63. Quoted in Jennifer Sullivan, "Police: Suspect Wanted to Join Singer's Family," *Seattle Times*, April 14, 2004.

64. Quoted in Jennifer Sullivan, "Lynnwood Man Arrested, Accused of Stalking Singer," *Seattle Times*, April 9, 2004.

65. Quoted in Austin Scaggs, "Avril Lavigne," *Rolling Stone*, June 24, 2004, p. 52.

66. Quoted in Davis, "Angelic Upstart."

67. Quoted in MuchMusic.com, "Transcript: Intimate & Interactive."

68. Quoted in Paisley Strellis, "Artist of the Month," YM.com, July 1, 2004. www.ym.com/stars/bandofthemonth/jul0104.jsp.

Chapter 5: Sustaining Success

69. Quoted in Ultimate-Guitar.com, "Lead Guitarist of Avril Lavigne Is Leaving the Band," September 13, 2004. www.ul timate-guitar.com/news/interviews/lead_guitarist_of_avril_ lavigne_is_leaving_the_band.html.

70. Quoted in MuchMusic.com, "Transcript: MuchOnDe-mand," October 18, 2004. www.muchmusic.com/music/ artists/transcripts.asp?artist=11&transcript=1.

71. Quoted in Rex Rutkoski, "Hear Her Roar: Avril Lavigne," The Inside Connection, Fall 2004. http://insidecx.com/ interviews/archive/avril.html.

72. Mike Ross, "Avril by the Numbers," *Edmonton Sun*, July 30, 2005. http://jam.canoe.ca/Music/Artists/L/Lavigne_Avril/ ConcertReviews/2005/07/30/1153855-sun.html.

73. Quoted in Joe D'Angelo, "Glammed-Up Avril Still Rocks Out," MTV.com, November 17, 2004. www.mtv.com/news/ articles/1493761/20041117/story.jhtml.

74. Quoted in Mike Bell, "Avril Bad Girl Turned Good," *Calgary Sun*, June 17, 2005. http://jam.canoe.ca/Music/Artists/L/ Lavigne_Avril/2005/06/17/pf-1092794.html.

75. Quoted in Steve Morse, "For Lavigne, Heavy Touring Makes World of Difference," *Boston Globe*, August 28, 2005, p. N4.

76. Quoted in Lesley Goober, "Avril Uncensored," *Cosmopolitan*, Volume 238, Issue 4, April 2005.

77. Quoted in Marc Weingarten, "Just Where Is the Next Stop on this Tour?" *Los Angeles Times*, August 11, 2005, p. E6.

78. Quoted in Rafer Guzman, "Lavigne Is Still So Complicated," *Newsday*, August 25, 2005, p. B5.

79. Quoted in Karen Bliss, "Lavigne to Shoot Movie with Gere," Jam! Showbiz Music, November 29, 2005. http://jam.canoe.ca/Music/Lowdown/2005/11/29/1329269-ca.html.

80. Avril Lavigne, "Dear Fans," AvrilLavigneBandaids, February 2006. www.avrilbandaids.com/images/avril_letter.jpg.

81. Haver, interview.

82. Avril Lavigne, "ALDO Fights AIDS—YouthAIDS," Youth AIDS-ALDO.org, 2006. www.youthaids-aldo.org.

83. Avril Lavigne, "Note from Avril About London Telegraph Article," Nettwerk.com, March 6, 2006. www.nettwerk.com/images/news_photos/70.jpg.

84. Quoted in *People*, "Avril's Happy Ending," July 31, 2006, p. 79.

85. Taylor, interview.

86. Sharifa Mohamed, e-mail interview by author, November 15, 2005.

87. Patrick Schabe, e-mail interview by author, March 28, 2006.

88. Quoted in Tim Cooper, "Rock & Pop: O Sister, What Art Thou? Teenage Girls Can't Resist Avril Lavigne's Sulky-teen Pose," the *Independent* (London), March 11, 2005, p. 17.

1984

Avril Lavigne is born to John and Judy Lavigne in Belleville, Ontario, Canada on September 27.

1989

Moves to Napanee, Ontario, where she will spend the remainder of her childhood.

1994

Transfers to Cornerstone Christian Academy in fifth grade. Sings first solo at Evangel Temple's Christmas concert. Plays in the boys' ice hockey league.

1996

Performs in local musical production of *You're a Good Man, Charlie Brown*.

1998

Plays a rebellious teenager in *Godspell*.

1999

Contributes to Stephen Medd's *The Quinte Spirit*. Wins radio station singing contest and performs onstage with Shania Twain. Meets Cliff Fabri, who becomes her first manager.

2000

Works with songwriter Peter Zizzo in New York City as part of a development deal from Nettwerk Records. Cowrites her first song, "Why," with Zizzo. Performs for Arista's L.A. Reid, who offers her a recording contract. Drops out of high school.

2001

Tries unsuccessfully to work with various New York writers on her debut album. Through Fabri, hooks up with Clif Magness and writes "Unwanted." Collaborates with the Matrix to create several songs, including "Complicated." Replaces Fabri with Nettwerk as her management.

2002

Releases debut album, *Let Go*. Wins MTV's Best New Artist in a Video award. Turns eighteen in September.

2003

Receives five Grammy nominations; wins none. Receives six Juno nominations and wins four awards. Begins her "Try to Shut Me Up" tour. Starts writing material for her next CD. Releases *My World* DVD.

2004

Receives three Grammy and two Juno nominations, but does not win. Plays a mall tour in North America with lead guitarist Evan Taubenfeld. Releases second album, *Under My Skin*, in May. Starts "Bonez" worldwide tour in the fall.

2005

Wins three Junos for *Under My Skin*. Becomes engaged to Deryck Whibley in June. Finishes her worldwide tour. Provides the voice for a possum character in the animated film *Over the Hedge*. Lines up two movie roles in *The Flock* and *Fast Food Nation*. Signs with the Ford Modeling Agency.

2006

Performs at the Olympic closing ceremonies. Appears in glamorous photos in February's *Harper's Bazaar*. *Over the Hedge* is released in May. Works on third CD. Marries Deryck Whibley.

For Further Reading

Books

Joe Thorley, *Avril Lavigne: The Unofficial Book*. London: Virgin Books, 2003. Contains an in-depth look at Avril's *Let Go* years, along with many color photos.

Kathleen Tracy, *Avril Lavigne: A Blue Banner Biography*. Horkessin, DE: Mitchell Lane, 2005. Brief biography covering her childhood through the release of *Under My Skin*.

Periodicals

Gavin Edwards, "Avril the Teen-Pop Slayer," *Rolling Stone*, August 8, 2002.

Elysa Gardner, "Avril: Adult but Still Herself," *USA Today*, May 24, 2004.

Daphne Gordon, "Nothing Complicated About Avril's Story," *Toronto Star*, June 4, 2002.

Jennifer Graham, "It's Not Easy Being Avril," *Teen People*, Summer 2004.

Shirley Halperin, "Avril," *Cosmo Girl*, June/July 2004.

Jill Kipnis, "Organizers Hope Lavigne Trek Has Happy Ending," *Billboard*, October 30, 2004.

Benjamin Nugent, "The Authentic Girls," *Time Canada*, July 8, 2002.

Rina Omar, "The Real Avril," *New Strait Times* (Malaysia), January 31, 2003.

David Segal, "Avril Lavigne, Unvarnished; In a World of Pop Polish, Ragamuffin Rock," *Washington Post*, January 14, 2003.

Bill Werde, "First Napanee, Now the World," *Rolling Stone*, March 20, 2003.

Internet Sources

Mike Bell, "Avril's Got A New Attitude," *Calgary Sun*, July 29, 2005. http://jam.canoe.ca/Music/Artists/L/Lavigne_Avril/2005/07/29/1152525.html.

Karen Bliss, "Avril Lavigne's Dark Side," *RollingStone*, April 1,

2004. www.rollingstone.com/artists/ourladypeace/articles/
story/5936982/avril_lavignes_dark_side.

CTV.ca News Staff, "Lavigne Still Adjusting to Some Parts of Fame,"
CTV.ca, February 28, 2003. www.ctv.ca/servlet/ArticleNews/story/
CTVNews/20030228/avril_lavigne_030224/20030228.

CTV.ca News Staff, "Under Our Skin," CTV.ca, April 20, 2004.
www.ctv.ca/servlet/ArticleNews/story/CTVNews/20040420/c
anadaam_lavigne_feature_040420/20040420.

Joe D'Angelo, "Avril Lavigne's No Wimp in a Tight Half-Shirt,"
MTV.com, June 27, 2002. www.mtv.com/news/articles/1455421
/20020627/story.jhtml.

Gil Kaufman, "It's Not 'Complicated': 17-Year-Old Avril Lavigne
Was Born to Rock," MTV.com, May 21, 2002. www.mtv.
com/news/articles/1454441/20020521/lavigne_avril.jhtml?
headline.

Sean Moeller, "Being Avril," *Quad-City Times*, September 25,
2005. http://ads.qctimes.com/articles/2005/07/21/entertain
ment/music/doc42df318ec319c593634473.txt.

Strawberry Saroyan, "Drop the Attitude," *Telegraph* (London),
February 26, 2006. www.telegraph.co.uk/fashion/main.
jhtml?xml=/fashion/2006/02/26/stavril26.xml.

Heather Stas, "Avril Lavigne: Too Much Too Young," VH1.com,
July 11, 2002. www.vh1.com/artists/news/1456027/0710
2002/lavigne_avril.jhtml.

Web Sites

Avril Lavigne Bandaids (www.AvrilBandaids.com). Her largest
fan-based Web site includes forums, sixty thousand photos,
and two thousand articles.

AvrilLavigne.com (www.AvrilLavigne.com). Provides content
such as news and photos. Her official fan club, CrossBonez,
is now free to join.

MTV.com (www.mtv.com). Search for Avril Lavigne in the artist
section of this American music site to watch videos, view
photos, and read numerous articles about her.

MuchMusic.com (www.MuchMusic.com). Search for Avril Lavigne in the artist section of this Canadian music site to read
transcripts, see videos, and access news articles.

About the Author

This is Yvonne Ventresca's second book for Lucent, following *Careers for the Twenty-First Century: Publishing*. Yvonne has written a number of freelance articles and is currently working on a middle-grade novel.